In a fast-paced, fast food society, confronting globalization, terrorism, and war, relationships are in danger of rupture and fragmentation. This is a wonderful book on the care of relationships.

Helen LaKelly Hunt
Author of *Faith and Feminism*

. . . A wise, tough, compassionate book about women's friendship. Joy Carol has skillfully woven together stories and probing questions of the many, richly diverse women whom she has interviewed.

Margaret B. Guenther
Author of *Holy Listening*

For every mother, sister, daughter, friend and colleague who has known the joys and sorrows of female bonds—and for the men who love them—this book is for you.

Deirdre Felton
Certified Thanatologist, international lecturer
on issues of loss and recovery

Joy Carol has the solution for the issues and emotions that we face in life—build healthy and lasting friendships! Her book is a great addition for all of us to strengthen our skills for living.

Pat Pearson
Speaker, business coach, therapist,
and author of *You Deserve the Best*

Every paragraph . . . will touch a nerve in the reader. We find ourselves in these pages and realize . . . we are not alone in our quest for answers to relationship puzzles.

Carole Barnes-Montgomery
Nebraska poet, *Nebraska Life,*
Plains Song Review, The Fence Post

Joy Carol deals with women's friendships . . . in a way that both celebrates their gifts and confronts their demons. She . . . is always gently pressing, gently prodding, gently questioning us—so that we can become better friends to one another.

The Reverend Dr. Nora Tubbs Tisdale
Author of *Making Room at the Table*

Joy Carol intertwines research with the personal stories. Her writing is clear and insightful, always helping the reader move toward greater understanding, transformation, self-acceptance, and good relations.

Barbara Hamilton-Holway
Author of *Evensong* and *Who Will Remember Me?*

Compelling interviews, stories, and illustrations make the many often unexamined issues in friendship come alive. This guide will enhance the relationships you have and set the stage for future ones.

Nina H. Frost
Principal, The Vocare Group and author of *Soul Mapping*

. . . A complex and rich tapestry . . . to be mined for inspiration, comfort, challenge. . . . Thanks to Joy Carol for honoring what women have always done: tell our stories.

Mary Zepernick
Former U.S. Section President,
Women's International League for Peace and Freedom

A thought-provoking page-turner on the depths and complexities of women's friendships. As I flew through the pages, I found myself rethinking my relationships with the most important women in my life. . . . A gift to treasure and, may I suggest, share with your girlfriends.

Emily P. McKhann
Author of *Living with the End in Mind*

In a market overloaded with articles and books about "how to get and keep your man," Joy Carol wisely redirects our attention to questions of how women strengthen and nurture one another.

Ruth L. Boling
Author of *Mouse Tales:*
Things Hoped For and *A Children's Guide to Worship*

Joy Carol intimately captures the essence of what every woman experiences: our lifelong development and journey mirrored in the women's relationships we choose to nurture or relinquish. For so complex a topic, her wonderful book concisely offers insights and guidance, with a genuine passion for women's healing.

Dorothy J. Papadakos
Composer and Lyricist

THE FABRIC OF
friendship

Celebrating the Joys, Mending the Tears
in Women's Relationships

JOY CAROL

SORIN BOOKS  Notre Dame, Indiana

© 2006 by Joy Carol

www.sorinbooks.com

ISBN-10 1-893732-95-9   ISBN-13 978-1-893732-95-7

Cover and text design by Katherine Robinson Coleman

Cover photo © Image 100/Alamy

Printed and bound in the United States of America.

Library of Congress Cataloging-in-Publication Data

Carol, Joy, 1938-
   The fabric of friendship : celebrating the joys, mending the tears in women's relationships / Joy Carol.
      p. cm.
   Includes bibliographical references.
   ISBN-13: 978-1-893732-95-7 (pbk.)
   ISBN-10: 1-893732-95-9 (pbk.)
   1. Women—Psychology. 2. Female friendship. 3. Interpersonal relations. I. Title.

HQ1206.C268 2006
302.3'4082—dc22

2006016899

Dedicated with gratitude and admiration
to the amazing women who shared their inspiring stories
and to the many women who have deeply touched my life—
my mother Alma,
my sister Shirley,
my niece Sheryl and her daughters
Natalie and Emily,
my goddaughters,
and my special friends.

Some friends play at friendship, but a true friend sticks closer than one's nearest kin.

Proverbs 18:24

A friend is one who knows you as you are,
understands where you've been,
accepts who you've become
and still, gently invites you to grow.

Anonymous

CONTENTS

ACKNOWLEDGMENTS

This book has taken me on a special journey into new and interesting places with the most astonishing people. It has given me fresh insights about aspects of women's relationships that I didn't know existed. I feel like I have received a wonderful gift. Behind this book are some exceptional people who helped me find the courage to interview and write about the joys and problems of women's friendships and how they can be enriched, improved, and transformed.

There are many people for whom I'm deeply grateful. First and foremost, I want to thank each one of the women whom I interviewed. They openly and courageously shared their transforming stories—including some rather painful and difficult ones. By their examples, these women have shown us how we can have stronger relationships, be better friends, and find joy and hope in our friendships.

I'm especially grateful for the blessing of my dad, Wilson Haupt, who was one of my greatest supporters. He was always there at any time of the day or night to listen to me read a paragraph or to rant and rave about my frustrations, concerns, and joys concerning the book. Half way through my research and writing, he departed this earth. I was stunned at the incredible amount of pain I experienced. It was then that I truly came to understand how helpful and powerful friendships can be, especially when we are in our deepest grief. I am thankful for that revelation. I also give thanks to my family and friends who are there for me when I need them and whom I appreciate more than they can possibly know—especially my sister Shirley and her daughter Sheryl; my reassuring reader friends Pamela, Joanna, Helen, Susan Joy, Ellen, Ginny, Katrina, and Carol, who lovingly read through many chapters and gave helpful comments; my friends Lou and Jane who did some great editing and cheered me on; my guardian angel Rosemary who continues to watch over me; the Union Center for Women, the Willard Sorority, and my many friends who persist in showing endless enthusiasm and support for my books.

I feel particularly blessed by the extraordinary people at Sorin Books/Ave Maria Press who encouraged me to write this book and had the vision to see the potential for it. I am most appreciative of the leadership and support of Bob Hamma, my superb editor, whose steadfast assistance and perceptive insights have bolstered me during its writing.

I thank each and every one of you; there is no greater gift that you could have given me than your support and belief in this book.

PREFACE

Researching and writing this book has been filled with joyful surprises for me. When my editor and I first talked about the book, I thought I knew almost everything there was to know about women's relationships. After all, I had founded the Union Center for Women in New York City over thirty years ago, I had been a women-in-development specialist in countries around the world for over three decades, and I had been involved with women's relationships and issues in the United States since long before the Women's Movement began. But I was absolutely wrong. I've more than doubled the information, knowledge, and understandings that I had earlier about women's relationships. And I've come to see and value whole new aspects about women's friendships that I didn't know existed.

When I started working on this book, I expected the focus would be on what made women's friendships so powerful and special. As I began interviewing women and exploring the research and literature on the subject, I soon realized that there are many misunderstandings that exist about women's connections and interactions with one another that have an effect on their relationships. Women's friendships are some of the most intense relationships in the universe—both in terms of their positive, supportive aspects as well as their negative, problematic characteristics. Women's relationships can be vital, growth-producing, fulfilling, and joyful; but they can also be difficult, painful, and damaging. They can make you laugh or smile, and they can move you to tears and anger. It's amazing what women's friendships can do.

As I continued interviewing women and digging deeper into the research, I heard stories that included useful lessons about women's relationships that I thought should be shared with both women and men. I began to ask questions: What do we really mean by "women's friendships"? If women are healthy and strong, are they better friends? Why do some friendships seem to weather the changes and storms of life and increase in value? Are there problems that come up in women's relationships that are fairly common? When problems occur, have women been able to transform them into positive experiences? What realistic solutions have women discovered and effectively undertaken that changed difficult situations? Can women learn to handle feelings of envy, competition, or anger constructively?

This book includes research findings, opinions, and ideas that focus on these and other questions about women's relationships. Scattered throughout every chapter are real-life stories of women's experiences from many cultures, races, ages, and religions.

In the chapters that follow, the women's stories validate the potential power of women's friendships. They also point out that when difficulties arise, it is possible to find solutions to problems, that women can transform themselves and enrich their interactions with one another. The women in this book provide us some valuable illustrations of how we can choose to experience the joy and power in women's relationships. They give us hope that we can learn how to have healthy, authentic friendships that will serve us well.

At the end of each chapter are some questions and ideas that came out of my discussions with women. As we talked about some of the complexities and obstacles that often emerge in women's friendships, I asked if they had understandings or experiences that had helped them when they were faced with dilemmas or problems in their relationships. Many women willingly shared ideas and strategies that they had found useful in resolving their difficulties. These suggestions are not to be considered as easy how-to advice or fix-it solutions. Rather they are questions and thoughts to help readers think of possible ways that they can approach and resolve any hurdles or concerns that they face in their unique situations.

Writing this book has given me the privilege of meeting many special women across the United States and throughout the world. I feel grateful that they were willing to talk with me about their experiences. To honor their anonymity, I have changed their names. Every one of their stories is filled with lessons that can speak to us and help us. They show us how we can strengthen our friendships and find the real meaning of being a good friend. They also show how we can mend any brokenness that may occur in our relationships with women and how we can be truly authentic friends.

No matter what your age, if you are a woman from thirteen to one hundred-three, there will be a place in this book where you will see something about yourself, about your relationships, about your hopes and dreams regarding your friendships. And if you are a man who is sensitive and caring and wants to understand more about women, I hope you will read this book and learn more about us.

As you read this book, I invite you to think of other stories, other lessons and approaches that might be helpful to you and other women who want to affirm and strengthen the power of women's friendships. Together we can reclaim the power of our relationships.

THE GIFT OF

friendship

ONE

When you have to walk that lonesome valley and you have to walk it by yourself, your girlfriends will be on the valley's rim, cheering you on, praying for you, pulling for you, intervening on your behalf, and waiting with open arms at the valley's end. Sometimes they will even break the rules and walk beside you. Or come in and carry you out.

Anonymous

I f I were to name something special that I would want to give to every woman on earth, it would be the gift of a healthy friendship with another woman. Women who have strong, genuine friendships feel accepted, affirmed, supported, sustained, and loved, even in the most difficult times. Indeed, authentic relationships between women are enjoyable, beneficial, and powerful—almost breathtaking. It doesn't get much better than that.

Women's friendships have a unique quality that may only exist between women. Melissa, a manager in her fifties, describes it this way. "I have wonderful relationships with men, and I'm married to John who has been my best friend for years. But he can't take the place of my women friends. They *share the same kinds of feelings* that I do, and we *talk about* those feelings. We look at the problems of life in the same way. When something goes wrong, my women friends *understand* what is happening; they know how I feel."

Laura, a journalist who is thirty-five, has another explanation for the irreplaceable power of women's relationships. "It's simple. Women and men tend to live their lives and see the world in very different ways. Women are emotionally and physically different than men. Women menstruate and can give birth. Although I love and need men, I also need people in my life who share things in common with me, who can relate to what I'm going through—and that's my women friends."

Many women talk about how it's easy to slow down, lighten up, and relax when they are with their women friends. According to Elizabeth Berg, "I relax about my attractiveness, in the broadest sense of that word. I feel accepted as I really am. I can eat garlic, reveal the fact that I'm wearing torn underwear, commiserate about certain ineptitudes. Most important, I can tell my stories and feel that they are heard and appreciated."[1]

There's also the sexual attraction between men and women. According to Ruth, a twenty-nine-year-old financial planner, "I find it difficult to have 'regular friendships' with men like I have with women. The relationships I have with men are often based on our sexual interest or attraction. If we act on that, we get involved in a romantic relationship, which is another completely different thing. If one of us isn't interested in a sexual relationship, we usually end things. I've only had one real friendship with a man that lasted after our sexual attraction ended." Perhaps only another woman can really feel in her guts what it means to be a woman. So relationships between females have an added bonus, a kind of purity and integrity, of someone who really "gets it."

Girls, and later women, can discuss anything or nothing; most subjects aren't off limits. They talk about growing up, about their dreams, possible careers, boyfriends, their sex lives, potential children, their fears, even death and dying. And most girls and women can find sheer pleasure in doing crazy things together and laughing about almost anything. I remember giggling with my girlfriends until the tears ran down our faces over the silliest incidents: a teacher's wig sitting lopsided on her head, a pimple that popped out on my friend's face just before her big date, worrying about being in an accident when we had on our old underwear, not realizing spinach was stuck between my teeth when I was trying to impress a really attractive guy.

Yes, women's friendships are special for many reasons. When friends are tried and true, they are there for each other whenever they are needed, to share their triumphs and failures, their laughter and tears. They want the best for each other, and they encourage one another to pursue their dreams and to find fulfillment in their lives. A quality friendship between women offers ongoing support, learning experiences, validations, mirrors of truth, confidence, a superb check and balance system. A good girlfriend clearly sees her friend for the person she is. She knows that her friend is a magnificent and valuable human being, and she tells her that if and when she needs to hear it. But she also lets her know when things don't seem quite right with her, when she is messing up. She jogs her memory in case she forgets who she is. Author Sue Monk Kidd puts it this way, "Our relationships with other women are part of the ground of our being. We discover ourselves through our girlfriends; it's a mutual process of self-discovery that goes on when we enter into this kind of female relationship."[2]

For many women, the company of their friends feels like healing balm; just being in each others' presence can be enough. They don't have to worry that they will be misunderstood or disliked if they are too powerful, too weak, too attractive, too unattractive, too smart, too simple, too successful, too much of a failure, too funny, too serious. Real friends allow each other to be completely themselves. They know who each other really is and still accept and love one another. And they feel confident that their relationships will weather all kinds of differences, changes, craziness, and transformations.

Experiencing this kind of caring makes women have courage to step out on a limb, try new experiences, and stretch their wings. Certainly a healthy friendship helps girls and women grow in every way. Jane Howard writes in her book

Families[3] about "friends of the heart" as people who can see the better sides of one another, who can enjoy their silences and their times of celebration. Such friends are not just polite and courteous toward each other; they are kind and bighearted too. Yes, this kind of friendship is one of life's extraordinary gifts.

In the last decade, numerous research studies have been undertaken documenting that solid friendships among women help them have a better quality of life. A long-term Nurses' Health Study undertaken by the Harvard Medical School[4] confirms that women who have strong female friendships lead happier and healthier lives than those who don't, and as they grow older they develop fewer physical health problems. The study points out that if women have close friends when their husbands die, they recover more quickly and rarely suffer from additional health problems. In contrast, those who have no friends are more inclined to be in bad health as a result of the stress caused by their husband's death. It was concluded that if women don't have friends, their health could be at risk, almost as much as if they smoked, were overweight, or didn't exercise.

Without a doubt, our female friends are extremely important to our emotional and physical health. They are precious and valuable to us, a real treasure. But, like everything in life, our friendships will eventually disappear from our lives because our friends move, have new commitments, become ill, or die. So appreciating our friends and savoring every minute of our time with them—while they are still in our life—is important.

Regrettably our friendships can also have problems. Sometimes it's simply that we've taken them for granted and allowed them to deteriorate. Or we've become too busy with "more important" matters. But that's not the entire story; there is more. When I randomly ask people to talk about their experiences related to women's friendships, I receive many diverse responses. Most begin with heartwarming, inspiring stories. Then they may pause and ask if I want them to include the experiences that are not as pleasant. Here are some of the less positive responses I've heard from my informal surveys. Women's relationships are often complex, challenging, and not entirely trustworthy. Women can be catty, gossipy, critical, revengeful, passive aggressive, and hostile. Sometimes interactions between females are charged with envy, competition, backstabbing, and misdirected anger. Moreover, women may be unwilling to say what they really feel or need, or they may disappear from relationships because they are unable to deal with problems that come up. At times they are unclear about boundary and control issues and disrespectful of the female sex—and consequently of themselves.

That's not exactly what we might want to hear, and it's definitely not the pleasing thoughts about women's friendships that were mentioned earlier. So how can this be? Generally we think of women as gentle, calm, kind, compassionate, and considerate. What would make their relationships so complicated or difficult?

As I searched the literature, I found numerous books about women's friendships—the wonders and power of them, as well as the problems and pitfalls. Phyllis Chesler interviewed hundreds of women, read thousands of studies, and took twenty years to research and write her book, *Woman's Inhumanity to Woman*.[5] In it she concludes that women's envy, competition, recrimination, and miscommunication can be found in all class, race, and age groups around the globe. In research studies undertaken in nineteen countries on five continents about the subject of women's attitudes toward each other, the findings reveal that indeed there are many women who do not respect, like, or trust other women, although *they may initially deny this*. While they are usually not as physically or directly violent as men, women can be aggressive in more indirect ways, and their anger and aggression is usually targeted at other women and children.

None of this comes as a complete surprise if we put this information in perspective. For centuries women have been viewed as second-class people, not nearly as valuable or as worthy as men. They have been treated poorly by cultures and societies, by institutions, by men, and by other women. We know that men and women who live in the same environment are affected by the predominant standards and ideology of their society. Psychologists and historians point out that women, not unlike others who have been exploited and demoralized, *accept, internalize, and even practice* the established views, standards, and repressive traditions of their culture. Without being aware of it, women may have *negative attitudes about their own sex and, consequently, about themselves,* which is often reflected in how they treat one another in relationships. Many women do this unconsciously without reflection; they are unaware of their behavior. Others may do this for their survival or to better their own status.

Furthermore, until rather recently, most societies have perpetuated—in both subtle and obvious ways—the concept that men are superior and may therefore dominate, make the decisions, and get the jobs. A man was expected to be successful in the world, and a woman was supposed to find a successful man who would take care of her. A woman needed a man to provide her with almost everything she didn't have: safety, security, and status. So for centuries, most women have been the "low man" on the totem pole, and as a result they have not been highly valued by men—nor by women themselves. Thus it is understandable that women might not trust each other, have negative attitudes toward one another, and treat each other poorly.

In my experiences growing up and as a woman, I've had to deal with some less-than-affirming judgments about me along with a few unkind and undeserved injuries inflicted by girls and women. And I confess that I too have been both a reluctant and willing contributor of actions that have caused harm to other girls and women. So although we know that women's friendships can be magical and rewarding, we also understand that they may be complicated and can easily get off track or go astray. In order to have strong friendships that don't disappoint us or slip away, we need to be aware of the possible pitfalls that can damage our relationships, of the unexpected glitches that can pop up in our interactions and can take us by surprise. When we are clear about potential problems and how and why they appear, we can develop solutions that will help us protect and nourish our relationships.

The chapters that follow review some of the problems that can emerge and wreak havoc in women's friendships as well as explore the reasons why they take place. I share strategies that creative women have developed, ideas which might help us deal with complex issues that transpire in our relationships. Good friendships between women are far too special and valuable to let them be damaged through carelessness, misunderstandings, mistakes, disagreements, or confusion. If we cherish, support, nurture, and protect these wonderful treasures, we may find that we have been given a special gift: a window into the soul of another woman.

• •

When we have a friend who encourages us to be ourselves, who loves us as we are, we have an incomparable treasure.

Alexandra Stoddard[6]

OUR MOTHER

our first friend

Becoming a better friend with your mother ... in
a very basic way, is the beginning of becoming best
friends with yourself.

Jan Yager[1]

For most of us, our mother was our first friend. Our mothers gave birth both physically and emotionally to us, their daughters. They provided us with our earliest experiences of love, satisfaction, and security. They also shared with us our first frustrations, disappointments, and hurts. The mother-daughter bond, which is almost always initially based on love, is probably one of the most important relationships we will have in our lifetime. No other connection will have a greater effect on us than this one. Indeed, whatever we experience in this relationship will probably be carried with us in some way throughout our entire life. After all, our mothers are our first tutors, and they teach us about friendship. When our "friendship" with our mother is positive, we will likely learn to be good friends with others. Because of the significance of this friendship, it is helpful, therefore, to understand the impact of our mothers' role as our first friend and to familiarize ourselves with the unique dynamics of this extraordinary relationship. In this way we can learn how to protect, build up, or improve it. Or we may want to make our relationships with our mothers more viable and affirming. We can do this by acquiring knowledge and tools to assist us in fostering and maintaining constructive interactions with our first friends, our mothers, and therefore with our relationships with other girls and women, our second friends.

In nearly every society around the world, mothers customarily carry the major obligation of nourishing and providing a safe environment for their daughters' growth. At a very early age, most daughters learn from their mothers how to be caring, giving, nurturing, receptive, and empathetic. Mothers also establish the milieu in which girls are prepared for their life within the culture. They introduce their daughters to expectations, traditions, and ways of life. They model and lay out most of the norms and standards for them to follow.

At its best, mother-daughter love can be caring, generous, unselfish, compassionate, uncontaminated. But because mothers are human and have both strengths and weaknesses, the mother-daughter relationship is not always at its best. As mother-daughter authors Julie and Dorothy Firman write, "Being a daughter and having a mother is one of the most profound experiences of a woman's life. It can be a wonderful, empowering experience or a frightening, disabling one."[2] A woman's earliest interaction with her mother will influence how she relates to other women. When there is much pain in this relationship, it can have a negative effect on a daughter's ability to trust and appreciate other women.

Undoubtedly difficulties between mothers and daughters can and do crop up—even in the healthiest of relationships. After all, mothers are human beings with their own insecurities, vulnerabilities, and sets of needs that are influenced by psychological, social, and economic circumstances often beyond their control. This will have a profound effect on their daughters' development. For example, when daughters express their need for contact, support, or independence, there will be times when their mothers will be able to reach out to them with encouragement and compassion. However, if the mothers' own requirements for security or fulfillment are not met and their self-esteem suffers, they likely will be unable to respond to their daughters in caring, sensitive ways. Indeed, they may react with frustration, anger, even hostility. When this happens, it can be extremely frightening to their vulnerable daughters, who may feel confused, insecure, even rejected. Certainly this phenomenon can occur with all mother-child relationships, but it is almost inherent with daughters, because mothers have a tendency to project themselves onto their daughters. As they identify with the frustrations and desires their daughters express, they may be reminded of their own childhood, of the boundaries and limits they experienced as girls, or of their own unmet wishes and needs.

Perhaps one of the most difficult dilemmas that all mothers and daughters have to face is connected with the complications and mixed emotions they experience related to their strong desire to have sound relationships with each other while trying to balance the daughters' dependency needs versus their requirements to become independent. Sometimes that balance is never reached, and daughters learn from their mothers that self-sufficiency and autonomy are not acceptable, that it is best if they adjust to the demands of others. Some daughters become so attuned to others' needs that their own go unmet. Girls who are mainly rewarded for being considerate of others may feel self-conscious and apprehensive about expressing their own wishes or requirements. They may repress those feelings as inappropriate. Therefore, when they later become involved in other relationships, they may be afraid to leave them even when they are unhealthy.

Sandy's domineering and needy mother rarely rewarded her for her good behavior or her accomplishments. Instead she punished Sandy if she didn't pay enough attention to her, calling her an ungrateful and disappointing daughter. Sandy spent much of her childhood trying to figure out ways to please her mother. By the time she was an adolescent, she was convinced that she was a mediocre, incompetent daughter. Now at twenty-three, Sandy has finally rebelled and separated herself from her mother. But she has carried her fear of rejection and her reactions to her mother's demands into her friendship with Annie. She is totally devoted to Annie who, like Sandy's mother, is extremely controlling and generally directs her life. Although Sandy feels the relationship is constricting, she believes her own needs must be denied. She is terrified that if she expresses them, the relationship will be threatened. Thus their friendship is seriously limited and laden with guilt.

Nancy Friday writes in *Our Mothers/Our Selves* about the subject of women's guilt, which she believes stems from relationships with critical mothers. "We introject the critical mother inside ourselves and carry her around in the form of her restrictive rules for the rest of our lives. We turn the anger at her against our self. It no longer is mother who denies us this, says no to that. We do it to ourselves, and if we break any of her rules, even if she does not know it, our overly strict conscience punishes us for her with feelings of guilt."[3] Certainly we acquire guilt from other sources, but when compounded by a mother's power, our guilt can be quite severe. Sadly many women suffer from the ongoing belief that they are always at fault, that they did something wrong, and therefore they must be guilty.

For decades there has been an interest in trying to understand the basics of this powerful, somewhat baffling mother-daughter relationship. In her book *Women and Their Fathers*, Victoria Secunda writes about how different the mother-daughter relationship is from that of mothers and sons, that no matter how independent and self-sufficient a daughter tries to become—even if she leaves her mother and family—the recollection of her mother's opinions and verdicts about her will always be a part of her personality and her character.[4] The emotional connection might not be observable, but it has the power to whip the daughter back to her mother almost like a bungee cord.

At some point in their normal development, most daughters begrudge their mothers' power over them and resent feeling needy or dependent on them. In their desire to have their own separate identity, they might reject their mothers, sometimes cruelly or angrily denouncing them. Later they discover that their mothers, whom they thought of as all-powerful, have very little authority in the outside world, and they realize that they too will grow up to be women without much worldly clout or influence. Psychoanalysts Judith Lewis Herman and Helen Block Lewis write that a daughter's feelings of worth can be damaged when she realizes that she too has the same "inferior status" as her mother and that her mother, like other females, prefers men over women.[5]

On the other hand, mothers, who are also daughters, may suffer from feeling that they are unimportant, undervalued, nonsexual. They can be jealous of their daughters' capabilities and potential, their freedom, the possibilities for doing things they never were able to do. They might even resent their daughters' happiness, their chances for fulfillment, their relationship with their fathers, their youth, bodies, sexuality. As daughters begin to develop their own identity and become independent, mothers may experience the sting of rejection. If it appears that their daughters are leaving or surpassing them, some mothers consciously or unconsciously inflict guilt and shame on them. Sometimes when mothers are insecure, have poor self-images, or are badly scarred or abused, the mother-daughter relationship becomes painful, even destructive. Some mothers turn their pain against their daughters by being disapproving, insulting, and cruel. Others brutally cut their daughters off or rigidly control and bind them to themselves through harassment, condemnation, and bullying. Unfortunately, daughters who are abused often turn into abusive mothers—as well as unhealthy, even hurtful friends.

When mothers are very destructive, their daughters may try to avoid being hurt by hiding their good qualities, their talents, and strengths. As a result, they grow up doubting themselves and holding back their own growth. Betsy Cohen writes that "envy from your mother is the most frightening kind of all, because you need your mother to make you feel safe and loved. From an envious mother, you learn 'Don't feel too good, be too good, look too good, do too well' or you will be envied."[6]

As we continue to explore the multifaceted relationship between mothers and daughters, we can easily comprehend that, even though mothers and daughters are biologically related to each other and share the same gender, their interactions will not always be easy, comfortable, or healthy. In fact, their relationships will likely have challenges and complex issues throughout their lives. Phyllis Chesler describes how the dynamics of this relationship can "profoundly influence how adult women treat each other. Psychologically, no matter how old they are, most women continue to (unconsciously) experience themselves as daughters and all other women as potentially benevolent, withholding, or threatening mothers."[7]

A daughter's earliest interaction with her mother often determines what kind of relationships she will have with women. Undoubtedly wholesome mother-daughter relationships teach daughters constructive behaviors that have a positive effect on their future friendships. On the flip side, unhealthy relations impart detrimental behaviors that can have a negative effect on women including excessive longing for acceptance, closeness, and support; being overly concerned about separation; being obsessed with the desire for security. Daughters who have experienced harmful relations with their mothers often worry that they are not good enough at pleasing someone, and they may become depressed or passive-aggressive because their own needs aren't being met. This can sabotage their own, as well as their friends', requirements for self-sufficiency and independence.

As they develop friendships, many women reconstruct relationships similar to the ones that they had with their mothers. If it has been positive, they tend to build strong friendships. If it has been painful, they may attempt to repair the hurtful elements they experienced with their mothers by developing close friendships with women who show some kind of motherly love or tenderness toward them. Others may be afraid to have a friendship that permits them to have the independence they were not allowed to have with their mothers. Some women abruptly cut off relationships with women who they believe are too strong or too weak, like their mothers.

If we want to have powerful relationships with our first friends, our mothers, as well as with other women, we need to disconnect ourselves from damaging and unrealistic impressions we've had of our mothers since we were children. Otherwise we will look endlessly for the perfect love we wanted but didn't receive from them—and which we will never get from our women friends. If we divest our mothers of some of those images and allow them to become real human beings— just like we are—with weaknesses and strengths, we may be able to relate to them in ways that are more constructive. By accepting our mothers for who they are, including both the special gifts they have given us and the baggage they inherited from their mothers, we can begin the process of healing our disappointments, hurts, and guilt. Perhaps we will become more realistic and truthful in our relationships with each other and be able to develop healthy and loving friendships with our mothers, who were our very first friends.

For years I've thought about the relationship that my mother and I had. Alma Johanna Weilage Haupt was a beautiful, gifted woman whose mother had come over from the "old country" in Germany. Mother raised two daughters, my sister Shirley and me, grew our vegetables and fruit in a huge garden and orchard, canned food for the long winters, butchered chickens and other animals, and sewed almost every stitch of clothing we wore. She also helped our father in the fields of our Nebraska farm. She seemed capable of doing almost everything from playing the piano to teaching Sunday school to growing beautiful flowers to baking the best apple pie west of the Mississippi River. What a model! I have often compared myself to my mother's accomplishments. Regrettably, I never became a great cook, my sewing attempts were not noteworthy, and I didn't progress very far with piano lessons. Whenever I evaluate my attempts at gardening, I wish my mother would magically appear with her astonishing green thumb. In small but significant ways, this probably has made me feel like I have not measured up.

Over the years, Mother and I had a reasonably healthy relationship. From time to time we had our disagreements and run-ins. Sometimes they were difficult and painful. I'm certain I disappointed her many times by doing my chores slowly and sloppily, by being a tomboy, by skipping Bible school classes, and by dilly-dallying around when she badly needed my help. Occasionally she punished me for being mischievous. Much later, I'm sure I disappointed her when my husband and I were divorced, and we didn't produce any grandchildren. It must have been particularly tough for her when I moved a long distance away from Nebraska and worked with impoverished people in developing countries around the world.

Looking back, I believe I unconsciously undertook those demanding jobs in desolate places because I hoped I would win more of my mother's respect and appreciation. Later, I lived in what my mother considered the rather treacherous city of New York. I'm still not certain if I moved away from her in order to become more independent or to separate myself from her religious strictness, her criticism of some of my actions, and her high expectations. I wonder if I thought I'd never be good enough for her.

When my marriage ended, I felt quite vulnerable and wounded. I was angry with a number of people and with God. For several years I wanted little to do with religion. I even stopped attending church services for a while. During one visit my mother made a few sharp remarks to me about being worried about my soul and where it might end up. Her words seemed judgmental and hurtful, and they cut me to the quick. I remember feeling upset, unsupported, and misunderstood. But rather than talking it over with her and trying to help each other understand what was happening, I withdrew and tried to distance myself from her.

Eventually I came back to Mother, and we grew very close. When she was ninety-five and still sharp as a tack, I got up my courage to ask her what she had meant by the words that had caused me such agony and if she was still concerned about my soul. She looked quite shocked. "Did I really say that? Oh, my stars, I guess I could have. I'm so sorry. Can you forgive me?" When I assured her that she had long ago been forgiven, Mother asked, "Now is there anything else I've said to you that we should discuss and get out of the way?" We cleared the deck of our unfinished business—on both sides—and forgave each other. We laughed at how absurd it was that I had not brought up this "problem" much earlier. We ended our discussion by Mother reciting my favorite nursery rhymes and singing a song she had sung to me as a child: "I have a little shadow that goes in and out with me, and what could be the use of him is more than I can see."

That night I helped Mother get ready for bed since my dad, who was her usual caregiver, was a bit under the weather with a cold. Mother decided to say her prayers in German, her childhood language which I did not understand. After she finished, she translated the words to me: "If I have done anything bad today, I didn't mean to do it. Please forgive me. May I wake up and have another chance to be good. If I should die during my sleep, take me home to you." We kissed good-night. Early the next morning, I flew back to New York City. The next day, my mother had a massive stroke and slipped into a deep coma. We never had another chance to talk again. She died a few days later.

I am eternally grateful that I talked with my mother about our unfinished business and that I was willing to face the possibility that she might be critical of me or that she might still think that I was not up to her standards. By approaching each other with kindness, openness, and a willingness to forgive and move on, Mother and I met each other on a level playing field of compassion, and I was left with a sense of peace and harmony. As time has passed since her death, I have come to see Mother much more realistically and to understand what she went through as a girl, as a young woman, and as an older woman. I now appreciate and respect who she was and who she will continue to be for me all the days of my life. Interestingly in this process, I also have begun to understand myself better and have found that my relationships with my women friends are richer and healthier. Today I accept and value Mother's perfectionism, her critical eye, her meticulous and hardworking principles, her fears, her love of beauty, and her zest for life—the parts of her that I hope will live on in me.

Valuing Our Mother, Our First Friend

• •

We can transform the mother/daughter relationship and we can transform ourselves. For every
woman who experiences the pain of the
mother/daughter relationship there is the prom-
ise of finding the joy.

Julie Firman and Dorothy Firman[8]

As I talk with women about their interactions with their
mothers and daughters, I ask if they have good ideas that
might enhance their relationships with one another, or if they
have possible solutions to help them when they experience difficulties. Many women have tried out ideas that have strengthened their relationships, making it easier to resolve any
problems they might face. These suggestions could be beneficial and encouraging for other mothers and daughters as well.
Some women have grown up without their birth mothers present in their life due to death, illness, adoption, internment, or
other reasons. They may have had a "mother-daughter relationship" with another woman such as a grandmother, aunt,
sister, friend, foster mother, or neighbor. I hope they find these
ideas of use to them too. Other women may have been hurt by
their mothers' mental illness, depression, alcoholism, or
abuse, which might have had a destructive impact on them.
When this happens to us, we may want to consider also seeking professional help.

*Is it possible that you may be just
like your mother—or your daughter?*
• •

Although most women find this difficult to comprehend,
our mothers were likely scared out of their minds about being
our mothers. They, too, were uncertain about what they were
doing, and they made a lot of mistakes in child-rearing.
Although our mothers probably wanted to do the right

thing—just like we do—they may have felt clueless about what to do when we needed them. If we can recognize and grasp this concept, it may make it easier for us to put our relationships with our mothers in a more positive perspective, and it might facilitate our reaching out to one another with greater compassion and ease.

Are you open to clarifying and
being realistic about expectations?

The roles of both mother and daughter are encumbered with off-the-wall expectations that neither one can possibly meet—especially the role of mother. Society has loaded the decks with crippling and unfair assumptions: "If only a mother didn't work" and, "If only she could do a better job of disciplining her children." Many mothers still assume the main parental role of nourishing, encouraging, restricting, and punishing children even when they are working full-time or fathers are present in the home. Therefore, if children's behavior appears to be "bad," mothers are often blamed. So, mothers and daughters, we may want to base our expectations of each other on reality. When we are able to see one another as the people we truly are with our human limitations, weaknesses, and strengths, our relationships will almost certainly grow stronger.

Can you define and respect your
uniqueness and your differences?

It's beneficial for both mothers and daughters to identify who they are and how they are different from one another. Separating out what are our experiences, our personalities, and our uniquenesses can be illuminating and growth-producing. By differentiating ourselves from one another, we are more likely to respect each other as autonomous women who are within an interdependent relationship. We might start by clarifying for each other our beliefs, values, practices, and issues. If we can accept our uniquenesses and our differences, we are on the way to having more compassionate and respectful relationships.

Does learning more about your mother make a difference?

Because we were raised at different times and places, our mothers have been exposed to and influenced by cultures and backgrounds that are quite dissimilar from ours. By gathering information about our mother's milieu, her history, her family and ancestors, as well as the illnesses and problems in the family, we will learn how these actions and events affected her. We may discover that our mother, like many other women, was trapped in a very limited and restrictive life, and that she had far fewer choices when she was growing up than we have today. We may better understand how she interacts with us and how we might want to respond to her—perhaps with more empathy and kindness.

Are you aware that most mother-
daughter relationships are imperfect?

Mother-daughter relationships are open to error, doubt, and ambivalence. After all, mothers and daughters are human beings who make mistakes and don't automatically like each other just because they are biologically related. Both suffer from feelings of loss, fear of being cut off, distress about control issues, envy about the other's position, and a lot more. Mothers may resent their daughters' capabilities, potential, freedom, and the possibility for doing things they never were allowed or able to do. They may feel the pain of rejection as their daughters develop their own identities and move away from their mothers in order to become independent. Daughters may dislike their mothers' strictness, control, and power over them, even as adults. As we begin to recognize this, we are on the path to having a more honest relationship.

Is it possible to listen and affirm
rather than blame and condemn?

Every woman I interviewed said it isn't productive or helpful to be critical, to argue with our mothers or our daughters, or to tell one another what they have done "wrong" or how they should do something "right." This creates a "no win" situation and causes the other person to be on the defensive, to protect herself, and to fling back arrows loaded with allegations and fury. Listening with an open and compassionate mind to the other person without *expecting* them to slip up, admitting one's own responsibility for blunders, and providing examples are all better ways to work out problems.

Are honesty and truthfulness possible?

My friend Joanna says, "There's trouble around the corner if you try to cover something up or soft peddle it." Truth *with love* is always better. Saying truthful words that are hurtful probably won't help, but modeling genuine, honest behavior that is considerate and kind can be beneficial. Some daughters remarked how valuable it was when their mothers said, "I'm human and I make mistakes. I may not be able to be everything that you need or want me to be. We might have to reach out to others to help us get through the challenges ahead."

Can you be compassionate and try to forgive each other?

When mothers and daughters learn to be compassionate with each other, they give each other a gift laced with empathy and kindness. They also help each other avoid and escape traps of anger, hostility, and resentment. Compassion opens the door to possible forgiveness and reconciliation. Whenever this occurs, it is enormously healing. Although it can be difficult, we may want to try forgiving the hurts we have inflicted on each other. Archbishop Desmond Tutu writes, "because we will hurt especially the ones we love by some wrong, we will always need a process of forgiveness and reconciliation to deal with those unfortunate, yet all-too-human breaches in relationships."9

This also applies to those who are stepdaughters and stepmothers. Occasionally we are given the gift of a child or of "another mother," and if we look at each other with more forgiving eyes, perhaps there may a blessed relationship there, too.

Can you change some things
and accept other things as they are?

There are many problems related to mother-daughter relationships (and to being female) that are difficult and complex.
Some can be changed or fixed, but many of them cannot.
Trying to repair things that are "unfixable" will only exacerbate the situation and will likely leave us feeling frustrated,
misunderstood, and angry. Each person has to make a decision
for herself about what she wants to accept or what she wants
to change. But we can't do it for each other.

Are you open to reconnecting with each other?

If we have completely broken off relationships with our
mothers or our daughters, we may want to explore possibilities
and options for a resolution. In most situations, it's better to
find a way to connect with one another, even minimally.
Making an effort to do so can prevent us from later suffering
feelings of guilt, remorse, and sorrow. Although relating to one
another may be painful, complicated, and far from perfect, it
might be worth the effort for us to reach out and try to establish some kind of connection with each other, if at all possible.

Are you aware that change
takes patience, energy, and effort?

Changing a difficult mother-daughter relationship requires
lots of courage, motivation, staying power, and determination.
Occasionally a transformation can happen, but it is usually a
slow process. If it occurs, the outcome might not be what we
expected or it may be different from what we wanted it to be.
But it can be wonderful and worth the time and effort.

* *

By working on the task of reconnecting with our
mother, we can bring to this relationship a greater
degree of self and can learn to appreciate the
"separate self" of this woman we call mother.

Harriet Goldhor Lerner[10]

OUR SISTERS

our partners in
friendship

THREE

Is there any relationship more lasting and complex and more capable of resolve than sister-to-sister? Our parents die, our children leave, we can separate from our husbands and lovers, but a sister remains part of us.

Barbara Mathias[1]

Sisters! The dream of sisterhood! Little girls and women who don't have sisters fantasize what it would be like to have a sister. They imagine having a sister who always loves them, who knows them inside and out. They yearn for a special relationship with a devoted sister, who shares everything with them, who will be there through the ups and downs. They know of sisters who are best friends, who do things together and are deeply connected. They hear powerful stories about how sisters rarely turn their backs on each other even if they feel ambivalent about one another; how they almost always return to each other even if they've been separated. They trust that sisters profoundly care for one another even if they dislike each other.

Our sisters have an enormous and lasting impact on our development and on our being. No matter how close or how distanced we may be, our sisters are permanently connected to us in some almost inexplicable way. Although we may be totally different from one another, we have shared the same mother, we were raised in the same family, and we are women. Our sisters are like extensions of ourselves; they can act as mirrors for us, they can be our shadow, our alter ego, our "other self."

In all probability our sisters know us better than anyone else does. And we will always feel drawn to our sisters for support and strength whenever we find ourselves in trouble.

Certainly I can personally vouch for the deep connection and loyalty of sisters, especially during tough times. When a neurosurgeon told me the frightening news that I had a brain tumor, I immediately phoned my sister Shirley who lived on the other side of the United States and told her the devastating news. I admitted how frightened and vulnerable I felt. I believe Shirley started packing her bag before I hung up the phone. She helped me prepare for the surgery, held my hand as I was wheeled into the operating room, and was in the ICU as I woke up. Although she had not slept for several days, Shirley seemed to be always with me, reading to me, massaging my back, or telling me the latest news until she was confident that I was no longer in danger and would surely recover. Yes, that's the dream of sisterhood we all long for and sometimes have.

But the reality of sisterhood can be quite different from the dream. Often relationships between sisters are filled with complications and far from perfect. Some sisters expect too much from one another; they want perfection, so they don't accept each others' flaws, imperfections, differences. Thus, they are often disappointed and critical of one another. As Carmen Renee Berry and Tamara Traeder write: "*Sister* seems to imply so much—on the one hand, a potentially devastating, sad relationship of discord and regret, and on the other, a closeness that no other relationship can offer."[2]

Many sisters experience endless struggles with one another. In my interviews with twenty-five women about their relationships with sisters, nearly half of them said something similar to what thirty-three-year-old Lily expresses: "My sister and I share a deep, rather complex love for each other. Although we are closely bonded in an intense, somewhat dependent relationship, our contacts with each other are often flawed by envy, competition, or disapproval. Occasionally we get very resentful and angry with one another." Of course, intensely dependent love relationships can also stir up competition, hostility, and conflict.

In her book *Between Sisters*, Barbara Mathias writes that we "have a low tolerance for our sisters' differences and idiosyncrasies. The underlying reason is in our gender, which is both a blessing and a curse. Girls grow up to define themselves in relation to others; but we also learn not to differentiate fully from others, not to claim autonomy without risk, and not to raise our voices loudly or aggressively for fear of losing love. And yet, when our sisters don't fit the mold of our expectations and conventions, we are critical and judgmental."[3]

One of the most common problems that sisters encounter is their competition to win their parents' love and acceptance. Although most siblings have to deal with problems of jealousy and rivalry, sisters seem to be affected more. If one sister appears to get more parental attention or is complimented more than another, the other sister may believe that she is less valued or not as loved by the parents. If one sister is successful and is praised, another may try to undermine her in an effort to make her look less worthy in the parents' eyes. Ginger, a twenty-eight-year-old school teacher in Florida, told me, "My sister has all the luck. I feel like our parents have always loved her more than me. Everything seems to work out for her— from the way she looks, to the man she married, to her success on the job. I try hard to look good around our parents and do special things for them, but they still seem to prefer her over me. When my sister is around, I feel intimidated and annoyed with all the things she does."

Although most sisters live with rivalry and fighting over who has the best or most of something, this dilemma seems to be magnified in small, nuclear families where there is only a set of parents or a single parent. Having an extended family of grandparents, aunts, uncles, and other family members nearby offers a protective buffer and takes some of the pressure off parents who have to provide all the acceptance, appreciation, and approval that their children need.

Some parents, whether unconsciously or consciously, create problems between daughters by setting them up as rivals who compete with each other. Although some contention between sisters will always exist, certain parental actions are likely to exacerbate problems between daughters, especially if they:

- favor one daughter over another;
- compare their daughters with each other;
- give privileges to one daughter and not the other;
- stereotype their daughters;
- neglect reassuring their daughters;
- lecture their daughters rather than help them work through problems;
- act as if there is no rivalry between their daughters;
- pay little attention to an older daughter when a baby sister is born.

Under the best of circumstances, the arrival of a new baby in a family that already has a child is like an assault or an invasion on the incumbent child's life and territory. This is particularly difficult for girls, because they are not supposed to object or complain, but rather to be pleasant and nice. Marie was born in the 1960s during a time when her parents were in transition. Her father had just lost his job and they were moving to Toronto, where they had no family connections or acquaintances. They hoped to find jobs and a better quality of life for their family. For nearly seven months, Marie's parents searched for affordable housing and for employment that would pay enough to support them. During that time, Marie's father was diagnosed with tuberculosis. It was a stressful and taxing time for the family, and they felt anxious as they faced numerous worrisome challenges.

During the years after Marie was born, her parents were busy coping with problems that occupied their attention and energy. They had little time to focus on their daughter's needs. Four years later, prior to the birth of Marie's sister Alicia, things started getting better. Marie's father had landed a respectable job, his tuberculosis was under control, and the family lived in a small, comfortable house. Just as her parents were beginning to be able to pay more attention to Marie, the new sister arrived. When baby Alicia appeared with all of her special needs, Marie's shaky life felt under attack again. The sisters were destined to have a thorny relationship. Over the years, the younger sister tried hard to please Marie, but with little success. Marie still believes that Alicia invaded her turf and stole her parents' love from her. Unconsciously, she undermines her sister and is critical of her efforts to please. She even accuses Alicia of being deceitful and two-faced. Although they continue to struggle to be civil to each other, it is easier for them to avoid having interactions.

Literature is filled with stories of sisters' insatiable desire to win their parents' approval, how they try to harm each other, how they go to great lengths to distinguish themselves as superior. Many sisters brag to others about their sister's accomplishments, but they may find it hard to praise them directly for their successes. More often they will feel resentful, envious, or cheated. Jody and Barbara's parents often compared their daughters with one another as they were growing up. "Why aren't you a good student like your sister?" "Your sister always does her chores on time. What's wrong with you?" As fifty-year-old adults, Jody and Barbara still struggle over who can do things better than the other, and they now fight about lifestyles, beliefs, and their frustrations with each other.

What makes sisters' interactions even more explosive and hazardous is the fact that the relationship is permanent and life-long. Christine Downing writes that it is "one from which it is almost impossible entirely to disengage. The permanence helps make it the safest relationship in which to express hostility and aggression . . . the bond between same-sex siblings is very likely the most stressful, volatile, ambivalent one we will ever know."[4] That supposition is validated by Susana, a seventy-two-year-old Cherokee elder, who confesses, "I have no problem getting along with most people, even hard-nosed characters. I plead guilty, however, to having plenty of difficulties with my sister. Whenever we get together, it feels like sparks start flying. I don't understand why we can't get along. But after we've been together for a while, I feel tense and angry and usually end up with a raging headache."

Sisters who feel powerless in other areas of their lives may try to hold power over one another in ways that are not always obvious. To keep their sisters in line, they may mock or laugh at them, use sarcasm, scorn, withdrawal, and piercing looks. Sometimes they put down each other's choices in life and get upset if their sister decides on a different lifestyle. Yet very few sisters are able to admit that they are fervently competing with each other or are envious of one another. If they would "confess," it might be an important step in restoring their relationship.

Linda and Sonja are twins who grew up in Minneapolis in the late 1960s. As young children, they enjoyed each other's company and were almost inseparable. Although not identical, they insisted on buying the same clothes and wearing their hair in the same style. Their parents encouraged the twins to get an education and to pursue whatever careers and lifestyles they might want. Linda and Sonja chose to attend the same college. "In our senior year," Sonja stated, "Linda fell head over heels in love with Johnny, the captain of the basketball team. She lost all interest in her pre-law studies and barely passed her final exams. A few weeks after graduation, Linda and Johnny were married and soon after that she was pregnant with the first of their three children. She became a stay-at-home mom and never went on to law school.

"After college, I went to graduate school in architecture and became an architect. Eventually I moved to Chicago and joined a well-known architectural firm where I did quite well. Although Linda often bragged about my accomplishments, I felt there was always a tone of bitterness and envy in her remarks. She talked about my status as something she could never attain herself, and she insinuated that I had advantages she never received. Whenever I went home to Minneapolis to visit the family, Linda and I inevitably got into unpleasant, sometimes malicious, arguments about inconsequential things.

"Over the years as we matured, we started to mellow out a bit. When our mother began to have serious health problems, we realized we needed to be more connected with each other in order to face the challenge of caring for her. One late night when I was in Minneapolis, Linda and I sat at the kitchen table discussing our concerns about our parents and how we should deal with them. We recognized how essential it was for us to be united, to work as a team on the challenges ahead. Sometimes in the early morning hours as we talked candidly, we were able to acknowledge our fierce competition and rivalry. We expressed our sadness over the loss of the friendship and trust we had experienced as children.

"Over time, we made a commitment to stop criticizing and undermining each other and to start supporting each other. Eventually we realized we didn't have to be the same; it was okay for us to have different lifestyles. After our mother died, we still had some lingering problems to work through, but we knew we were moving in the right direction."

Because most women yearn to have a "good sister," they may look for them in their friendships. But the negative feelings women have for their blood sisters are often carried over into the way they interact with their friends. If they see their sisters as envious and resentful, they may perceive their friends in the same way. Some women choose friends who are completely opposite of their sisters in order to steer clear of the problems they experienced with them. Others select friends who seem comparable to their sisters. Myra, a twenty-nine-year-old woman in a small town in South Carolina, talks about her interactions with her sister. "Stacy and I have had a horrible relationship since we were little. So I intentionally chose a woman to be my best friend who is a lot like Stacy. I hoped my friend and I could work out the difficulties that my sister and I experienced and never could resolve. I wanted to prove that I was able to have a healthy relationship with a woman who was like my sister.

"Believe it or not, it actually worked. I tried out different ways of relating to my friend without getting emotionally riled up about the outcome. I didn't worry if I might threaten her or wouldn't be able to please her. By experimenting with my friend, I learned how to get out of the pressure cooker of emotional, knee-jerk reactions that I have whenever I'm around Stacy.

"One day I finally realized I *could* live without my sister's approval, that I wouldn't fall apart or die if she criticized or belittled me. Only then was I able to pull myself away from her strong grip on me. Little by little, I began to work at being more honest with her—and also with myself. Now I'm much less defensive, and I'm not afraid of her retaliation. I've been surprised to discover that this not only released me, but it changed how my sister and I react to each other.

"Oh, it's been slow going, and we move forward a little and then slide way, way back. After what has seemed a very long time, we are more able to approach each other as two completely different women who, by the way, happen to be blood sisters. Most of the time, we no longer feel compelled to compete for our parents' love and approval. A truly red-letter day occurred when we realized that neither one of us has to be 'the best.' Now when we are together we can be more the women—and the sisters—we really are. Actually, I think we're becoming friends, but it has been a long haul with lots of hard work."

These stories show us that sisters' relationships can be positive and, if problematic, improved, especially when the sisters have a willingness and an openness to work through difficulties. That's good news. And there's more. I've heard many incredible stories about sisters' loyalty and devotion, how they protect and fight for each other whenever anyone threatens them. Fifty-three-year-old Felicia, who lives in New Mexico, told this moving story. "I'm the youngest of three sisters. All three of us were born within a period of five years, so we are close to each other in age. We were very poor and didn't have many things, but our parents were loving people with great faith. They had high expectations and were quite strict about what kind of behavior was acceptable for us.

"Sometimes I think we became close because our parents required that of us. Early on they taught us how to care for one another, so we were more like three little nurturing mothers, rather than three sisters competing with each other. From our early childhood until now, when we are in our fifties, we have been very protective of each other. We've always felt that together we could take care of almost anything, that harmful people or destructive events couldn't have a huge negative impact on us.

"During some really rough times, our family was forced to become migrant workers. For nearly six years, we followed the crops across the southeastern part of the United States. It was difficult for the whole family. The work was backbreaking and demanding, and we had to be in the fields in the hottest weather. When my sisters and I were separated from our parents in the field, some of the male workers tried to make sexual advances toward us. The people who owned the fields didn't seem to care what happened to us. So we three sisters stayed close together and didn't allow anyone to harm us. I believe that experience made us even stronger and closer.

"Not long ago our oldest sister Alicia was diagnosed with cancer while she was going through a terrible divorce. We younger sisters took her and her kids into our homes and cared for them. Together we were like mother hens gathering our chicks under our wings and protecting them.

"I've been asked if we feel much envy and competition with each other. At times we have some of that, but it's not really malicious or nasty. Maybe it's because we have very spiritual parents, who set high standards for our behavior. My parents told us that they expected us to help take care of each other, that hateful or cruel fighting and rivalry were not allowed. Maybe it's also because we had so little money and very few possessions, so there wasn't a lot to fight over. We learned to create our own games and be a team.

"As I look back at everything that happened to our family and what we experienced over the years, I can say that we certainly had our share of problems. But our life has also been filled with lots of wonderful things: love, good health, friends, family, and sisters too. Yes, sisters can be a pain in the neck sometimes, but at other times they aren't. We should always appreciate them because they are a special gift in our life."

Felicia may be right. Perhaps we have too many things and are too materialistic. We may be envious of our sisters because they seem to have more than we do. Possibly we haven't received enough guidelines telling us what is acceptable or unacceptable behavior between sisters, so rivalry and competition run rampant in our relationships. But I really like what Felicia says: that our sisters can be a special gift in our lives.

Appreciating Our Sisters, Our Partners in Friendship

We are stuck with our particular sister as we never are with a friend ... the relationship is permanent, lifelong, one from which it is almost impossible entirely to disengage.

Christine Downing[5]

Our sisters can be wonderful friends and partners. That's something worth protecting or working toward. Women have tried out some interesting strategies to enrich their relationships with their sisters. Others have developed approaches to help clear obstacles and snags that occur in interactions with sisters. Some of these suggestions may work for you, or they might spark another idea. You may want to create and explore other options, too. As with solving problems in mother-daughter relationships, the task of restoring a complicated or troublesome relationship with one's sister requires patience and bravery. And you may also need a good dose of energy and empathy.

Do you value who you are as well as who your sister is?

Sisters are individuals with gifts, strengths, and weaknesses, who happen to be part of the same family. In order to relate well with one another, it helps enormously to know ourselves and feel secure about who we are. Then our sisters' attributes and accomplishments can be celebrated; they will not be seen as a threat to us. When we have a positive sense of ourselves, we can be more connected to one another in a constructive way. Perhaps we can begin by trying to see one another as we truly are, not as we want each other to be. By laying out clear expectations for our interactions based on what is realistic and fair, we will create a sound foundation upon which to build healthy relationships.

*Can you stop expecting your sister
to be someone you want her to be?*

This problem is often not acknowledged, but many women have incredibly high standards of what makes a sister *tolerable* or *acceptable* to them. If a sister does not meet their "requirements," they may feel disappointment, frustration, and anger, and they may even reject her. But sisters are not puppets; rather, they are women with their own needs and ideas about whom they want to be. Even though our sisters might not meet our unstated "requirements" for them, it's important to accept them for who they are and not try to make them into what we want them to be.

Are you willing to affirm your differences?

It's important that sisters not only identify who they are as individuals but also identify how they are different from each other. Although at times we may wish that our sisters would be more like us, diversity does make life more interesting—for sisters too. We can start by clarifying how we are different from one another and by telling each other about our personal beliefs, values, practices, and issues. Then we can affirm and celebrate our differences.

Are you willing to drop criticisms and accusations?

. It is unproductive and damaging to be critical, to blame, or to fight with our sisters. Telling them what they are doing wrong or how they should do it right is not helpful. Doing so usually causes our sisters to be defensive and protective of themselves, and they may react by pointing a finger and slinging accusations at us. Listening with a genuinely open mind, admitting our own responsibility if we have made a mistake, and practicing positive ways of caring for each other will create a better environment for building stronger relationships.

Can you validate each other's roles and experiences?

It's easy to make judgments about each other's roles and experiences—especially in relation to who did more work caring for parents, who had the most difficult situation in the family, who got hurt, who didn't get as much love. If we can acknowledge and validate each others' experiences, roles, and responsibilities and understand that these may be some of the causes of the difficulties in our relationships, then we can start to shorten the distance between one another.

Can you stand up for what you need and stop "suffering"?

Life is too precious, too short to be bullied or to be on the bottom of someone's foot. If our sisters are walking all over us and we continue to lie down and take it like a doormat, they will keep on bullying us. Perhaps we don't mind being walked on, but it can hardly be a healthy position. Indeed, making useless sacrifices is like betraying ourselves. Clarifying for our sisters—and for ourselves—what is important to us and what are our limits is a more helpful approach. And if we are the sisters who are doing the bullying, we may want to take note of this suggestion and make amends.

Can you admit your feelings and
end malicious envy and competition?

It's only natural that there is some envy and competition between sisters. But sometimes these feelings can become malicious. Cruel envy ends up going nowhere but to the junk-yard of negativity. Talking about feelings may be a good way to defuse potentially explosive situations and to take a step toward having a healthier relationship. Although it may be difficult to eradicate bad thoughts totally, they can be modified. Who knows? We may find ourselves laughing over the futility of having such unnecessary feelings.

*Can you benefit from examining
your early experiences or your history?*

Our sisters (and other siblings) are the only people on the planet who share the same genes, home, relatives, and family friends, and who really understand what it was like to have been raised by our parents. We have a connection that goes very deep. We may want to take a serious look at the impact of our family's history on our development. We can include such factors as our birth order, family size, status of our parents' marriage, their physical and emotional health, deaths in the family, social and financial influences on the family, any religious and cultural pressures. This process will help us have a better understanding how our roles in the family came to be, and how we have learned to react to each other. It might make it easier to change how we treat one another.

*Are you aware that relationships
between sisters are complicated?*

The relationships between sisters can be often complex and loaded with potential pitfalls. Many sisters suffer from feelings of inferiority, from a fear of being compared to another sister, from envy about a sister's position or rank within the family, from resentment about a sister's accomplishments, and more. Sisters often feel that their parents are unfairly giving more attention to another sister. Just because we are biologically related to each other does not mean that we will get along well or that we will like each other. Once we truly grasp this, we may recognize that our sisters are likely suffering from the same feelings and anxieties as we are. Perhaps this will help us feel more empathy toward each other.

Are you willing to change the things you can?

At times, problems related to relationships with our sisters may seem colossal. Some can be changed, but many can not. Trying to fix the "unfixable" only makes the situation worse and will leave us feeling misunderstood, annoyed, and further apart. Each of us needs to make our own decisions about what we want to keep or to alter in our relationships. But no one can decide to do it for anyone else.

Do you worry about doing things wrong?

We are our own worst judges. We always want to get things right, so we worry if they aren't. But worry is truly a wasted emotion with absolutely no positive results. It is possible to live our lives without worrying if we are going to do something wrong to our sisters or if we are going to be appreciated or envied by them for doing something right. After all, sisters are ordinary people who make mistakes, but who also do things right. Here's a strategy we might want to follow: Carry on with living as though we are normal human beings—which is what we are.

Are you willing to work at forgiving
and reconnecting with each other?

Restoring an unhealthy relationship with our sisters does take hard work and patience. If we agree that we want to improve our interactions, we will need to commit ourselves to devoting time and energy to developing a better way to connect with each other. We may want to explore all possible options for a solution, including apologizing for hurting each other. If we are able to forgive one another and then let go of our guilt and anger for what we or our sisters probably did or didn't do, it can be more satisfying than we could ever imagine. And if we do work things out, we will be grateful for having reached out to one another because the rewards are remarkable. Keep in mind that most women yearn to have a sister and to experience the power of sisterhood.

Good luck, sisters!

Our sisters hold up our mirrors, our images of
who we are and of who we can dare to become.

Elizabeth Fishel[6]

RISING ABOVE

envy

Envy is one of the biggest disappointments friends experience. Envy can creep in between best friends, just friends, friends who are similar or different . . . envy can accompany and threaten any friendship.

Betsy Cohen[1]

We all have feelings of envy at some time or another. We want to have our needs met, to feel satisfied, to feel good. Envy is a normal response when someone has something that we need or want. It is only natural that we will want to have it too. But sometimes this ordinary desire can become a serious dilemma in our relationships. There is always someone who has what we *think* we need: a better financial situation, a more supportive family, a nicer man, more trustworthy friends, a better education, a more meaningful job. Or we may *think* that we have to have what someone else has: attractiveness, energy, intelligence, creativity, confidence, admiration, material possessions. The list of needs and "have to haves" gets longer and longer, especially in highly competitive cultures where success, power, money, and materialism are sought after and valued. Before long, the green-horned monster of envy can take over, and the one who envies may feel ensnared in a web of deprivation, frustration, and misery. Desperation will cause some to go to great lengths to obtain the objects of their envy through courting, cajoling, attacking, belittling, and sometimes even by destroying the objects of their envy.

Because envy is such a powerful emotion, it has been judged as one of seven deadly sins. The word envy comes from the Latin word *invidere*—to look hatefully at someone. Envy is having a strong, perhaps hateful, desire for the privileges, position, possessions, or characteristics that another person has. If you envy a female friend, you want what she has and what you think you don't have: her success, her looks, her friends, her money, her family, her man, her home. Envy can sneak into any kind of relationship and wreak havoc. It is notorious for being a killer of women's friendships.

According to Ann and Barry Ulanov, professors at Union Theological Seminary, those who are envied become almost frantic in their attempts to defend themselves.[2] No matter what they do or how they try to explain themselves, an unfilled envier will not listen to them. If they try to reveal who they really are, they will likely be accused of boasting or of being condescending. On the other hand, if they give up on being accepted for the person they are, they may be criticized as being detached or distant. Someone who is envied may be like a prisoner held captive by an envier.

One of the problems related to envy is that society, and mothers in particular, usually teach women to be humble and self-effacing. We've also been told that if people see us as too successful, we stand the chance of not being popular or accepted, that some people might view us as a threat. What's more, we may be in danger of being attacked and hurt. Certainly that is less true in the years since the Women's Movement. But generally it has not been considered acceptable for us to talk about our strengths and accomplishments since we might be seen as bragging and could be labeled arrogant or presumptuous. As a result, we tend to downplay our achievements or pretend they didn't really happen. We don't want to be the target of someone's envy. In the past when I was complimented for an accomplishment, I said something like "oh, it was really nothing," or "I guess I got lucky." When I was named the Outstanding Young Educator of Colorado and later of the United States, I told people "they must have made a mistake." Looking back, I'm certain I downplayed my achievements because I was concerned about being attacked by an envier or of losing friends. In fact I have been wounded by enviers, and I'm certain I too have hurt people I've envied.

My fifty-six-year-old friend Betty is an outgoing, brilliant woman and a successful manager in the corporate world. Many women encouraged her to move up the ladder and become the head of a large corporation. When she succeeded, however, I was shocked at the reactions of some of her "supportive friends." They were jealous of her accomplishments and some became downright mean. They started backstabbing and gossiping about how she was acting "just like a man" in the position, how she wasn't as friendly or as available to them as she had been. It was as if they hadn't noticed that she was trying to run a male-dominated corporation. They didn't reach out to help her, but they were critical that she wasn't supportive of them. Soon they began to abandon her. It was a sad lesson on how a woman's success can breed toxic envy.

But lest we forget, let's remind ourselves that envy often backfires on the envier. When we are acutely envious of others or secretly want them to suffer, we usually end up hurting ourselves. The high cost of envy may include shame, guilt, loss of peace of mind, insomnia, even physical illness. There is an old saying that envy can do more damage to the jug in which it is held than to the object where it is poured.

Evelyn, who is thirty-nine and lives in Oregon, had a female supervisor in a research laboratory where she worked. "Dr. Smith was insanely jealous of my success as a researcher. I'm sure she was afraid I might be promoted to her position. She became obsessed with trying to guarantee my failure. One night she went into the laboratory and destroyed months of my research. I was devastated and terribly discouraged. I didn't believe I could get back to the place where I had been. When what Dr. Smith had done was discovered, she was released. Of course, word got out about her actions and she was unable to find another similar position. I understand she ended up a bitter, humiliated woman."

Sometimes when we look at another woman's life, we make assumptions that her life is better than what ours could possibly be. We imagine that she has what is lacking in our life. We may get upset, even angry with her and with ourselves. Perhaps we create an image of someone whom we can envy, so we will end up feeling bad about ourselves, almost like a form of self abuse or punishment.

Angie and Jennifer, two women in their mid-thirties from Maryland, had been friends for almost seven years. When Jennifer's husband left her for another woman, she felt rejected and despondent. Angie encouraged Jennifer to get out, to try new things, and to move ahead with her life. She made enormous efforts to support Jennifer, dedicating hours of her time, energy, and resources. But when Jennifer started going out on dates and getting involved with other friends and activities, her life was moving faster than Angie's. Angie resented that Jennifer didn't seem to need her anymore. After all, she still needed Jennifer. She felt Jennifer was abandoning her and leaving her behind. She complained to others that Jennifer had not recognized what she had done for her. She began to envy Jennifer's dates, her other friendships, her independence. Before long, Angie withdrew from the friendship and began gossiping about Jennifer's perceived disloyalty and her lack of appreciation for Angie's efforts. Inevitably, the pain of envy shut down what had been a supportive friendship for both women.

As children, most of us were taught by our families, teachers, religious institutions, and society that envy is bad and thus forbidden. We learned that we should be happy about other peoples' accomplishments and successes. So when envy pops up on our screens, we feel guilty or loathe ourselves for having such unacceptable feelings. Rather than trying to learn how to accept and manage this tyrant, we tend to deny that it exists. Or at least we try to hide it from others. Unfortunately, hiding envy doesn't work very well, and it too has a way of turning against us.

In attempting to conceal our envy, we may try one of many possible schemes—mostly unsuccessfully, I might add. Some of the most commonly used methods are what I think of as the easy "cheap shots": disapproval, criticism, gossip, backstabbing. We find a flaw or weakness in a woman we envy. By talking with others about her faults and devaluing her, we try to make ourselves look more important and her less so. For a while, we may even feel more "powerful." We criticize a woman as a way of undermining her. "She sure spends a lot of time doing volunteer work. Maybe she should spend a little more time with her aging parents."

Another ineffective method is acting as if we don't care about something and avoiding situations that are difficult for us. Consequently we suffer silently, usually alone. Josie, who is the caregiver for her twenty-six-year-old bedridden daughter in Pittsburgh, acts like she is not resentful that her friend Ida Mae is free to go out at night because she can afford to hire someone to help care for her elderly mother who lives with her. Sometimes Josie avoids seeing Ida Mae so she doesn't have to deal with the envy she feels about her freedom. Or she pretends that she is too busy, that she has something else going on, and she withdraws and quietly experiences her pain by herself. If someone asks her how she feels about this, Josie answers, "Oh, it really doesn't bother me at all." She becomes the silent suffering servant who seems not to care that her life is full of pain.

Perhaps we try another scheme similar to what thirty-nine-year-old Gerry from Iowa does: wallow in self-pity about the injustices of life. "Beverly always gets to do nice things like traveling to exotic places. I'm too busy to take a vacation. I have to stay here and take care of my parents who have health problems. None of my sisters or brothers are able to help, so someone has to do it." We can almost hear Gerry saying to herself: "It's not fair. Look how lucky Beverly is, look how bad things are for me. Poor me."

Or we try what we think no one is wise to: phony praise. How many times do we hear someone say something that does not ring true? "You look absolutely wonderful," when we are exhausted and look terrible. "You did such a good job," when in reality we barely made it through a presentation. Joyce, a twenty-eight-year-old professional musician, remarked, "What bugs me is when someone does something better than I do, and she doesn't even practice as much as I do. Then I go up to her and profusely compliment her when what I really want to do is strangle her. I wonder if she knows I'm not being sincere. But what's worse is that afterwards I feel guilty about not only being envious of her, but also for being phony about my praise."

Believe it or not, there can be a silver lining to the turbulent cloud of envy. Although it's not easy, this dark and difficult emotion can be transformed into something helpful, almost constructive. In her book *The Snow White Syndrome: All About Envy*, Betsy Cohen describes "The Continuum of Envy" as possibly moving from being destructive to being positive.[3] It begins with the detrimental *wish to harm* (our desire to see our friend suffer, to wreck what she has that we don't have) and moves through such feelings as *self-hatred* (hating our friend because of what she has, and hating ourselves for not having it), *resentment* (resenting our friend's good luck or fortune, which we think we will never have), *covetousness* (craving and longing for what our friend has and wishing it could be ours), *admiration* (although we may envy our friend, we think she did a good job and we wish we could do it as well), and ends up with the positive aspect of *emulation* (we may strive for what our friend has and possibly use her as a role model).

So at the destructive end of the continuum, we may experience feelings of anger, self-hatred, and despair. But if we can figure out how to move to the more positive side, we might end up admiring someone and trying to improve ourselves so we will be more capable of getting what we need or want. So envy at its best can be used as a tool, a way of learning what we want to do or become.

Carolyn, a quiet, forty-four-year-old nurse in Wisconsin, describes how it has become easier for her to be less envious of her friends' accomplishments and talents. "When I didn't feel good about myself, I felt overwhelmed with feelings of envy, especially if my friends were attractive, slim, energetic, or outgoing. When they told me about their travels or successes in their exciting jobs, I was jealous and angry about the things they could do that I thought I could never do. Then I felt awful and berated myself for having such thoughts. I would try to stuff down my feelings. Who knows where they went? But I'm sure they went inside me and made me anxious, insecure, and sometimes physically ill.

"One day my friend Judy, who is single and an accomplished business woman, admitted that she felt envious of my life, that she really wanted what I had: meaningful work, a solid marriage, a devoted husband, smart children, the ability to cook and throw a great dinner party. Well, I was shocked. How could she possibly envy me? I felt so ordinary and uninteresting, so overweight, so plain as compared to the way she was: slim, well-dressed, talented, articulate, successful. We ended up really hashing things out and finally laughing about both of us being insecure and having such envious thoughts.

"After that, I decided it would be good for me to start concentrating on what was good about me and what I had that might be an asset. I went to counseling for a while and was surprised to learn that I really am quite special. Now I'm starting to like and even enjoy myself. Also, it's easier to be more accepting of my friends—even the ones who are slim, beautiful, and successful. I've learned that I can choose whether I do or don't want to do something similar to what one of my friends does. After all, I too have a lot of my own good stuff."

Yes, Carolyn, you do. And your story is a reminder to all of us that we need to find our own "good stuff." Maybe then envy will not overwhelm us and harm our friendships.

Rising Above Envy

• •

Envy is, of course, the most serious obstacle to
friendship and bonding. In its worst form, it
ignores, denies the existence of the other.

Madonna Kolbenschlag[4]

Although we may not want to admit it, envy has a way of
sneaking into our lives at some time or another. If we make an
effort to recognize it before it gets out of control, we may be
able to reduce some of the potential damage that can occur to
our relationships when we get caught in the snares of envy.
Here are some suggestions for rising above envy that women
have been testing to release themselves from envy's grip.
Perhaps they will help you and stimulate other ideas too.

Do you value who you really are?

Like many women, we may spend a lot of time thinking
about the people we want to be, our ideal selves. Possibly we
compare that image to the person we think we are. We may
believe we are not good enough, so we are dissatisfied with
ourselves. Or we feel envious of our ideal selves, which we
think we see in the qualities of other people. Identifying,
understanding, and valuing the real people we are, our actual
selves, are helpful ways to find self-satisfaction. There's a good
possibility that we *are* better than what we *think* we are.

*Are you able to celebrate your
own successes and accomplishments?*

My mother often told me that there is only one person who
lives with me from my birth until I die—and that is me. Since
Mother was absolutely right about this, it's important for me to
learn how to like myself, enjoy being with myself, and compliment myself when I do something worth celebrating. There
might not be anyone else around to do that for me. When we
are able to enjoy and celebrate our own undertakings and

accomplishments, we probably won't be so envious of other women's successes, and we might feel liberated enough to honor them, too.

Can you stop comparing yourself to others?

Here's an interesting idea: In order to have envy, we first have to compare ourselves with someone to discover what we lack that they have. That's risky business and a sure way to expose ourselves to the highly contagious disease of envy. Making comparisons is looking outside ourselves in order to feel good or bad about ourselves. But no matter what we see, we still are who we are and the other person is who she is. It might be possible that we are comparing ourselves to someone who is comparing herself to us, and she may be envious of us. So we need to give ourselves a vaccination against making comparisons and start feeling good about ourselves on our own.

Do you respect and appreciate
other people's gifts and skills?

If we are not threatened or envious of our friends, we can truly appreciate whatever they bring to our lives. In some ways, it's like enjoying a good performance, a special walk, or a delicious meal. A smart woman, a talented mother, or a dynamic friend can all be gifts to us. So maybe we can just relax and savor them.

Can you use envy as a caution sign and a learning tool?

Although feeling envious of someone else really is a waste of our time, there may be a reason that we are feeling envious. Our life may not be what we want it to be. Perhaps we should stop and take a look at what we are envying. If it is something we really need to have in our lives or something we want to become, we may want to enrich our skills and talents. Perhaps there are things we should learn or improve. Maybe we want to develop new skills by going back to school, taking a language course, or getting training in a craft. Before my dad died . at age ninety-six, he reminded me that learning is a life-long process that should never end. He was still learning new words as he worked at crossword puzzles just days before his death. A bonus of learning something new is that it can dampen the fires of envy and make us feel better about ourselves. So we can use envy as a caution sign and a learning tool. In the end, we probably won't yearn to have what others have. And isn't that the ultimate goal?

Are you able to salvage friendships
that have been damaged due to envy?

If we have been good friends for some time or if there are special things in our friendship that we enjoy, it's worth making efforts to keep that relationship from slipping into the pit of dead friendships that went awry because of envy. We may want to ask ourselves how and why we became friends, what is good about our friendship, and what we enjoy about each other. If we can talk and laugh together, our friendship merits struggling for, and it just might outlive our envy.

Can envy be used as an
opportunity to strengthen friendships?

Women who have solid friendships can talk openly about their problems of envy. They are able to admit that they feel envious if the other person has qualities they want to have. Rather than feel guilty because they think "I wish I had what she has," they learn to accept that what each person has is unique and special, and to enjoy it. We might want to try talking about our feelings of envy with our friends. We may be surprised that it's not difficult to do, and there's no need to fear retaliation or worry about losing our friendship. In fact, the relationship may become stronger.

Are you willing to stop making assumptions?

If we think our friend has everything and we have nothing, we probably are making assumptions that are not based on facts or on the truth. We may be imagining things because we haven't had the opportunity to learn about the entire situation. Making assumptions is a foolish thing to do, and it rarely gets us where we want to be. So if possible, let's step back and put a good dose of reality into the picture. Chances are, we will be surprised at what we learn.

Can you steer clear of gossip,
destructive criticism, and backstabbing?

One of my professors in seminary said, "Never, never, never engage in gossip, rumor, hearsay, or backstabbing. It will come back to haunt you, only twice the size." And then she added, "If you ever feel the urge to engage in such lowly pursuits, run as fast as you can to a safe place and tell yourself the gossip, rumors, and hearsay *about yourself*. That should immediately cure you."

Are you willing to ask for help if envy is overwhelming you?

Some women have been seriously wounded by difficult situations and harmful people, and they lack self-esteem and self-confidence. If we are unable to get out of the quicksand of envy on our own or we feel it will consume us, we would likely benefit from having someone help us. It could be a friend whom we really trust or a counselor, therapist, pastor, or spiritual director. There are also support groups that can be helpful. We should not hesitate to ask for assistance; it could change our lives.

• •

Envy is a prime cause of the discontent many people feel about their lives. Yet we are so ashamed of envious feelings that we seldom pull them out into the light where we can get a good look at them.

Joyce Brothers[5]

COMPETITION IN

friendship

FIVE

Confidence and competition are critical tools for
success, yet they break the rules of femininity.
Openly competitive behavior undermines the
"good girl" personality.

Rachel Simmons[1]

Competition is a natural consequence of living in the
world. Every creature on the planet competes with
others in order to survive. As long as competition is
not hateful or out of control, it can be a means to inspire or
motivate people to improve. Although our society revolves
around independence and competition, women have not been
encouraged to be independent or to develop separate identities. Nor have they been taught how to compete openly and in
an advantageous manner. Thus when women find themselves
in competitive situations, they are uncertain how they should
act. Consequently, they are treated as second-class people and
have a difficult time thriving in this society. Even in modern
times, most women continue to stay within acceptable "regula-
tions" and roles: being pleasant, accommodating, selfless, and
noncompetitive. Because of this, women's competitive
impulses are often forced underground, where they may
become quite hazardous.

Not long ago, women's existence and survival were closely
linked to men's lives. Their position in society depended

almost entirely on the status and role of the men in their lives: first their fathers and later their husbands. Consequently, it was essential for them to find and connect up with the best possible men. Under these conditions and pressures, women naturally regarded each other as rivals who fought to get the attention and interest of men. Competition between women was serious business and was mainly focused on who was the prettiest, the best flirt, the sexiest, the sweetest. The sought-after prize? The most eligible and successful man (see "Men and Friendships").

But in today's world, competing for men is only one part of a much more complex story of competition. Soon after we are born, we begin needing approval and recognition from women much more than we do from men. As Luise Eichenbaum and Susie Orbach write in *Between Women*, "We have wanted our mothers' attention and have had to compete for it against other children, family responsibilities, outside work, or her separate interests. For girls especially, the loss of our mother's attention, which we have all experienced . . . often leaves girls feeling insecure."[2]

Throughout history, mothers and daughters have competed with each other to win approval, to be young and beautiful, to get more attention, to emulate each other, to be closer to the man of the house. They almost certainly have conflicting emotions as they grapple with their longing to be loving while experiencing competitive feelings with each other. In discussions with mothers and daughters, some talk about how they feel torn apart and guilty about their competitiveness, how they are aware that they may be hurting each other but seem unable to prevent themselves from competing (see "Our Mother, Our First Friend"). Thirty-year-old Joline from Chicago said, "When I was a teenager, my mother wore make-up and dressed up every day, even when she stayed at home. She told me it wasn't fair that I looked so pretty and young, that she felt old. One time she said that my dad thought I was more beautiful than she was. It made me feel terribly guilty, like it was my fault. So I worked at looking fat and ugly. But that just seemed to make her angrier. When I finally left home in my early twenties, I was loaded with guilt feelings that I had let my mother down, that somehow I had deserted her."

Another important aspect of competition related to mother-daughter relationships is that of sharing the same gender. Frequently mothers who do not have a clear and separate sense of their own identity try to find it through their daughters. Those daughters will likely have to struggle to establish their separateness. This is not as true for sons, who don't share their mothers' gender. From birth, boys usually identify themselves as separate and different from their mothers. By and large they search for their own identity by setting themselves apart from others, as compared to most girls who try to establish their identity by connecting themselves with others. Thus for men, competition calls attention to their differences, while for women, it may feel like a threat to their identity.

Sometimes mothers who are extremely competitive pass their competitiveness on to their daughters. Some try to compete through their daughters. I'll never forget listening to mothers talking outside a well-known ballet school in New York City as they waited for their daughters. "Isn't it sad how much weight Karina has gained?" "I don't think Debra has the right body for a ballerina." "I wonder why Zoe's mother pushes her to stay in the classes when she's not graceful." It felt like a deadly cock fight—or perhaps I should say a deadly hen fight. Sadly this kind of toxic competition is widespread and takes place all over the world.

Many women try to move away from the competition they experience with their mothers by developing close relationships with other women. Melody, a thirty-year-old insurance agent in Oklahoma City, told me that she was putting her trust in female friends. "My friendships with women have the added bonus of giving me a sense of confidence and security. Unlike my mother, I know my friends will not compete with me for popularity, attention, success, or men." But women friends can and do disappoint us. They may even abandon us, thus repeating and validating the rejection we may have felt from our mothers. As I talked with groups of women, many said they would not compete with their friends because of their fear of losing them. Some adamantly stated that competition with friends was unethical and unacceptable, that they would feel disloyal if they competed with them.

Elisa, a twenty-four-year-old Hispanic woman in Dallas, said, "For me, competition means that there is some kind of race taking place, like one person wins and the other one loses. My group of friends agreed that we should not compete with each other, because it would damage our friendships and harm the trust we have with one another. But most of us secretly compete with each other in some way or another. And we're not honest about that, because we're scared we will lose each other. So we lie and are deceitful, which isn't good for any of us. In the end we really mess things up."

In her book *The Secret Between Us*, Laura Tracy confirms this phenomenon saying that women hide their competitive spirits from each other because they are afraid that they might be seen as being unique or different from one another.[3] They are concerned that this will cause their friends not to like them and therefore they will be deserted. Perhaps this is the main reason women find it difficult to admit that they compete with each other. But by not acknowledging our competitiveness, we are being dishonest and, as Elisa says, we can "really mess things up." Moreover, we may be in danger of permanently damaging our friendships.

Unquestionably girls and women compete with each other for many reasons: popularity, attention, recognition, men, promotions on the job, status, power. Sometimes in highly competitive situations, they are capable of becoming cruel, domineering, dishonest, and hateful. If a female is seen as being too smart, too pretty, too popular, too successful, too gifted, too different, she may be the target of hostility, meanness, and bullying. It's rather common for female cliques to use brutal aggressive acts to control girls or women, to force them to submit to certain behaviors, or to stop them from competing. They may intimidate someone into compliance by backstabbing, shunning, gossiping, even ganging up on her and beating her. These aggressive actions can be extremely damaging to the recipient (see "Anger in Relationships").

Dee, a high school sophomore in Connecticut, described some of the ways girls attempt to hide competitive feelings to avoid being bullied by the "in" girls, with whom they long to be friends. "Yes, my friends and I are very competitive—almost cutthroat at times. But we're careful how we show that. When we talk to someone, we might say, 'I'm so ugly' or 'I'm so fat.' We want them to think we're not trying to be the prettiest or the skinniest girl—even though we probably wish we could be. Or we might say, 'I really hate you because you're so thin.' It's okay to say things like that.

"We don't dare say or do something that looks like we are challenging or competing with someone. If we get out of line, we are in deep trouble with the girls who are popular. And they can be tough. Sometimes they spread nasty rumors and lies about you, or they tell boys how bad you are and how they shouldn't be seen with you, or they just cut you totally out of the group. You might as well be dead."

After hearing stories like this, I'm glad I grew up years ago when girls in my high school in Lincoln, Nebraska, were less deadly with their competition. But maybe I've forgotten how bad it was. I know that when my family first moved to Lincoln from our farm when I was in the ninth grade, I was a naïve country girl wearing hand-me-down clothes without a clue about makeup, boys, girl talk, popularity, foreign languages, algebra, and all those city things. And I certainly was not one of the "in crowd." Of course, competition and friendship in that school were completely different from anything I had experienced in the country school I attended near Clatonia. In the first eight years of my formal education, I went to a one-room schoolhouse where there were a total of twelve to fifteen students in eight grades. My only classmate Dennis was my friend and constant companion. We didn't have a lot of choices or competition. Every student in the school had to play touch football, softball, and volleyball. It didn't matter how poorly we played. I was usually the last one to be chosen for softball because I was more interested in making dandelion chains in the outfield than keeping my eye on the ball. "Watch out, Joy! Ball coming your way." No, not a lot of competition!

So competing in the ninth grade in a city school was about trying to figure out how to survive the move from a tiny pond to what felt like a gigantic ocean, how to get someone to sit with me in the school cafeteria, how to make friends. Over the years, I survived and lived to tell the tale. I'm sure it was because some really kind girls adopted me as their "country-bumpkin" girlfriend (see "Surviving through Friendship"). I am eternally grateful to them. Eventually I figured out how to compete in "safer waters" by getting involved in various student activities and performing in school plays. I now know that those are healthy ways for girls and women to compete for approval and acceptance.

Rosalind Wiseman interviewed ninth grade girls for her book *Queen Bees and Wannabes.* "The amazing thing is that no matter the girls' race, geographic location, class, or religion, I always get the same answers. . . . They're all about competition, about looks, style, friends, popularity, and boys—things girls think they need to secure a place in the life raft."[4] These are some of the responses she received about what girls didn't like about their friendships:

- Talk behind your back
- Gossip about you
- Are two-faced
- Are jealous
- Are competitive
- Are critical
- Are judgmental
- Tell your secrets
- Are a tag-along
- Take your man
- Make you choose friends
- Betray you
- Are fickle

Not exactly how we might want to describe friendship!

Sometimes excessive competition is a camouflage hiding our deep need for someone to listen to us or to appreciate who we really are. When Amanda was growing up in Wyoming, her parents constantly compared their daughters to each other and only praised them for the specific qualities *they* valued in them. One daughter was regarded as smart, another as beautiful, and Amanda as reliable. Throughout her life, Amanda, who is now in her fifties, has been in endless competition with her sisters, trying to be appreciated for her abilities that she thought were never recognized by her parents.

Today women have more opportunities to enter and compete in new roles in society, especially within the work force (see "Working Well with Women"). Many women have bought into the concept that they should compete as aggressively and in the same manner as men. They may even attempt to duplicate what they see "successful men" doing rather than develop new, perhaps more appropriate, ways to compete. Lillian Rubin writes in *Just Friends* that women should become more skillful at dealing with competition, that for too long they have "been constrained from expressing their competitive strivings cleanly and clearly, that they become distorted into the kind of petty rivalries, jealousies and envy that sometimes infect their relationships with each other."[5]

Certainly competing carries a lot of baggage for women. No wonder it has been frightening for many of us to jump in the ring and participate in unguarded competitive activities. If we compete, we are saying that we are not the same, that we are different or better or worse. Thus we are acknowledging that we are standing alone. That may feel like a threat to our need to be connected. Rosemary, a forty-one-year-old accomplished cellist in San Francisco, could not handle being in competition with her female colleagues, who were also her friends. "I don't want to compete with my friends. I don't want to be 'better' than they are so I can get a job or perform. It's too uncomfortable for me. Even though I'm a good musician, I'm afraid I may have chosen the wrong career. So I've decided to teach students to play the cello rather than having to compete."

Perhaps it's time to change this picture. We know that women are capable of competing. But if they don't believe

that or they aren't given support to compete, they will continue to be anxious and insecure. What's worse, they will cruelly
act out their negative feelings through hurtful discrimination
against each other and against themselves.

It's encouraging to note that there are women who are carv-
ing out new ways to compete openly and healthily with other
women. Nora, a thirty-four-year-old teacher in Washington,
D.C., is a good example of that. "When I was in high school,
many of my friends were very smart, but we felt awkward
about competing with each other. I was careful not to tell anyone whenever I did well; I tried to hide my successes. When
my friends found out that I had won an award, they acted as if
they didn't like me or that I'd hurt them. I felt like I had to
apologize to them for doing well.

"After graduation, I lost track of my friends, and for a
while I only ran around with male friends. Their friendships
seemed freeing, more casual, healthier, and their competition
was easier and out in the open. With men I didn't have to
'look out' for them or worry about hurting their feelings. And
we didn't need to apologize to each other if one of us did well.

"Over time, I grew more confident about my skills and
strengths. When I competed, I could win or lose without getting terribly emotional. Then I started meeting some self-
assured and poised women for whom I have a lot of respect.
Eileen is a super mother, homemaker, and computer whiz; she
can do just about anything. Eva is a talented teacher at my
school who is respected by the teachers and students.

"It's great, because I no longer feel threatened by such talented women. I'm just pleased that these wonderful women
are in my life. We compete openly whenever we want, and we
don't have the need to put each other down or try to hurt one
another. This kind of competition helps me to stretch and
reach higher levels of achievement—but only if and when I
want to. I can also sit back, relax, and take pleasure in the wonderful gifts these friends bring to my life." Now that sounds
healthy!

Appreciating Competition in Friendship

● ●

It isn't that women don't have competitive feelings, only that they have much more difficulty in acknowledging them and, therefore, acting on them.
Lillian Rubin[6]

Although competition can be an unpleasant issue for many of us, there is good news. Women have tested out and discovered strategies for dealing with this challenge. Perhaps their ideas will give you thoughts about how you can compete in a healthier way and feel more secure as you do. And you might be relieved of some of the sting of uncontrolled or excessive competition.

Do you value who you really are?

We are all people of worth with our own unique qualities, strengths, and weaknesses. Once we understand that, it makes it easier to decide whether we want to compete or not. We will learn that it's okay to win at some things and to lose at others. And we won't need to go for the jugular or try to destroy someone who seems to be "better" than we are at doing something. That makes the playing field much more level for everyone. If we are able to accept just this one point alone, we will have moved miles away from the destructive aspects of competition.

Can you build up your strengths and your self-esteem?

Women with strong emotional, psychological, and spiritual qualities are usually not afraid of competition. That's why it's a good idea to know what our special skills and gifts are and to maximize them whenever possible. By improving ourselves, we naturally boost our self-esteem. With more confidence and self-assurance, we can then choose when and how to compete in ways that will make us feel comfortable and successful. As a result, we will be unlikely to continue experiencing the intense fear of competition.

Are you aware that competition can be positive?

Competition does not have to be destructive. It's not just about being the best, about beating someone, or about receiving the most kudos. Competition can be about learning from someone else's achievements and helping ourselves to move in a direction that will fulfill our personal aspirations. As we are able to compete more openly and without fear, we can overcome some of our feelings of insecurity and self-doubt. Then competition will develop into something that is much less cutthroat and more balanced for us.

Are you aware that competition
can be your need for recognition?

We all need to be recognized for who we are and for things we have accomplished. We also want others to perceive who we are as individuals, not just as part of a group, a team, or a family. So if we understand that we may be competing to receive recognition or to show off, it might make a difference in the way we compete.

Can you imagine your "rival"
having trouble with competition, too?

If we are threatened by the person with whom we are competing, we might want to imagine that person having the same feelings and insecurities as we do. In that way, we can relieve some of the pressure we feel and mellow out a bit. Perhaps we will learn to accept each other. Sometimes we are only competing with ourselves. If that's the case, we might want to take another look at this idea and apply it to ourselves.

Can you practice different competitive activities?

Various forms of competition may evoke different responses and feelings for us. We might find it helpful to experience assorted competitive activities such as dancing, singing, debating, and sports. By doing this we learn whether we like competing as part of a team or by ourselves. Knowing how we feel in these situations will help us choose appropriate avenues of wholesome competition. Some women don't feel comfortable competing in teams because they feel too exposed or too "blamable" by other team members should they mess up. Other women love teams because they feel less isolated, less "on stage" if they make a mistake. They know others will make errors too. So let's feel free to practice.

Are you able to lighten up when you compete?

Women are infamous for being extremely emotional when they compete, especially if they "lose." But wearing our feelings on our sleeves is not constructive. We might want to work at not getting overly emotional, at not being hurt if things don't go our way, or at not feeling left out. As a friend of mine says, "Lighten up and toughen up." It can help.

Can you learn from humiliating competitive experiences?

At times, competition can be painful and downright humiliating. When someone made fun of me because I didn't do well in a competitive situation, I was so embarrassed that I thought I'd never be able to pick myself up. Certainly I didn't want to compete again—ever. But when I look back at this experience and analyze what happened, it helps me to get over it and to move on. By allowing ourselves to look at and examine those times when we have been "hurt" in competition, it can be beneficial. It's a little like having an old wound that never heals properly until it is opened and cleaned.

As a parent, can you provide
support and respect for your daughter?

Daughters who grow up knowing they are supported and encouraged by their parents usually are able to compete in a healthy way. When they have the backing of their parent's love and respect, they feel energized and confident enough to develop their own unique identity—even when they are surrounded by gifted siblings and friends.

*Do you understand that other people also want to be
"the best"?*

The bottom line is that we are all just people who want to
feel good, who want to be "the best," even though we can't all
be the best every time. But that's okay too. We need to understand and accept that we live in a competitive world and other
people are competitive—just like us.

Women's feelings of competition are an expres-
sion of their energy toward life, toward self-
actualization, toward differentiation and the right
to be one's own person.

Luise Eichenbaum and Susie Orbach[7]

ANGER IN

relationships

Why does someone avoid expressing anger?
Because she is afraid that to express anger will
make others disappear, evaporate, reject her, and
not wish to be around her any longer.

Jan Yager[1]

We do not expect nor do we want women to be angry or aggressive; it is upsetting to us. So the topic of women's anger can make us uncomfortable and nervous, and we may want to change the subject. After all, women are supposed to be gentle, kind, and nice, certainly not capable of doing the cruel and violent things that men do, such as fighting, torturing, killing, raping, or making war.

When I ask people about this topic, their remarks are quite interesting. "I've never met any angry or aggressive women; they're too nice." "I often wonder why women who don't seem angry suddenly blow their top—usually at the wrong person." "Women's anger is a little like shadow boxing. You don't see it or know where it is until you've been hit by it."

Unquestionably, women can be and are angry, and there is no scientific or biological reason why they should be less angry than men. In most cultures, the real problems emerge because women are expected *not to show* such "unacceptable" feelings and are, therefore, forced to suppress them. Consequently, in order to be tolerated, a woman must hide or bury these emotions, likely somewhere inside herself (see "Recognizing Needs and Feelings").

Yet, as psychologists point out, harmful feelings that are not recognized and released have a way of ricocheting. I refer to this as the "overstuffed garbage can theory." If you endlessly stuff garbage into a can without removing some of it, it can get awfully hot and rotten in there. Eventually an explosion takes place, the lid blows off, and garbage is spewed all over the place. "An explosion" of a woman's unresolved anger translates into an eruption of actions that could be destructive to the woman herself and to others around her. They might include passive-aggressive behavior, false accusations, backstabbing, rumor mongering, gossiping, malicious secretive activities, even female sexism. Almost any of these acts have the potential to harm the life of a girl or woman probably more than straightforward anger or aggression.

Alexis, a forty-three-year-old dental hygienist in Boston, describes what happens when she is angry. "Since I was a little girl, my parents told me that I was not supposed to get angry or lose my temper; that behavior was not suitable for a girl. So when I get angry or upset, I don't know what to do with my feelings and I try desperately to ignore them. Then I start getting a pain in my throat, and I'm afraid I'm going to choke. I cry if anyone looks at me the wrong way. Everything seems out of control, and I completely lose my confidence. Sometimes I get very depressed and don't want to do anything. It's horrible."

Luise Eichenbaum and Susie Orbach write that we have two images of women related to anger. It is either "the contented, mother figure . . . unflappable, absorbs everyone else's pain and upset, and projects warmth and ease" or "the angry, nagging shrew . . . dissatisfied with her lot who flies into a rage at the slightest provocation."[2] Either one of these images leads us to conclude that women should not feel or show their anger. Eichenbaum and Orbach also point out that when female friends experience problems or disagreements, it likely will be difficult for them to express their feelings honestly or openly with each other. So when a dispute between women gets complicated and heated, there may be accusations, rage, and guilt, that cause tensions to become almost unbearable. This is terrifying for most women. It's not surprising that they avoid dealing with their feelings of anger or are unwilling to express them openly. But their trust in each other suffers and their relationships can easily be eroded.

Numerous studies have been undertaken that indicate that women's anger and aggression are quite common around the globe. Victoria Burbank, an anthropologist from the University of Western Australia, studied female aggression in 137 societies in Asia, Africa, the Middle East, South America, the Caribbean, and among native-American tribes in North America. She found that women were the targets of female anger and aggression in 91% of the societies studied, while men were targets in only 54% of them. According to Burbank, the targets were mainly sexual rivals, wives, "the other woman," and women whose relationships were not specified.[3]

In some cultures, open female aggression is not considered objectionable and is quite common. But in most cultures, girls and women are taught that they are not supposed to attack each other directly, but rather express these powerful emotions in ways that are considered to be "nicer," more fitting, less direct. Since most females have a strong desire to bond and have companionship with each other, they do not openly carry out actions that might be unacceptable because of their fear of rejection. Therefore, aggressive acts are usually undertaken secretly behind someone's back, and the aggressor can deceive herself that the victim will not know who attacked her. In *Woman: An Intimate Geography*, Natalie Angier writes about indirect aggression: "It is an aggression that we gals know, because we grew up as girls and we saw it and struggled against it and hated it and did it ourselves. Indirect aggression is anonymous aggression. It is backbiting, gossiping, spreading vicious rumors. It is seeking to rally others against the despised but then denying the plot when confronted."[4] It can also be shunning, ostracizing, and staring at someone with evil eyes ("looks can kill").

So why are female anger and aggression often directed at other women? There are many theories about this phenomenon, one of which focuses on women fighting each other over a man (see "Men and Friendships"). Another theory proposes that women are powerless prisoners within a patriarchal society and are compelled to be submissive to male-dominated structures and customs. Therefore, they are only allowed to express their anger at one another. At the other end of the spectrum is the concept that opportunistic women, of their own free will, actively enforce the rules (mainly established by men, I might add) that control and harm women. No matter what the reasons, damage and pain have been inflicted on girls and women for centuries.

As her son was growing up, Phyllis Chesler observed how anger and aggression are played out between young boys as compared to girls of the same age. She noticed that her six-year-old son and his friends wrestled with each other and often got into verbal and physical fights. But they didn't seem to hold a grudge against each other nor did they scheme against a third boy. As they grew older, they recklessly linked up with one another without much thought or without knowing each other well. On the other hand, Chesler observed that six-year-old girls were already deeply involved with "best" friends. From time to time they ended those friendships and quickly replaced them with new ones. Sometimes they attempted to turn their new best friends against the old ones. As the girls grew older, they were careful not to offend each other because they feared they would be rebuffed or, even worse, banned from their group. They were concerned that other girls might not approve of them. This constant need for approval made them more scheming, manipulative, and indirect, but also more apprehensive.

Chesler vividly describes the pain and devastation that girls and women experience when they are victims of indirect aggression or are excluded by members of their own sex.

"Unlike boys and most men, girls and women continue to socialize mainly with female intimates. Thus, when a girl or a woman is excluded by other girls or women, a more primal and painful terror is evoked. A friendship web, once severed, can rarely be repaired. The raw feelings of hurt and shame, the 'backstabbing' rumors, the betrayal of trust, the loss of one's reputation, the sudden falling away of human society, amount to a loss of one's own existential footing."[5]

Thirty-year-old Lisa, who grew up in Germany, talks about that kind of loss. "When I was growing up, my friends and I wanted desperately to belong. We had to have a best friend, a kind of guaranteed relationship. We wanted someone who would be there for us whenever we needed her. We would do anything to avoid being isolated. If one of our friends got angry at us and did something to hurt or upset us, we didn't dare tell her how we felt. We were too scared she might say something nasty about us or reject us. Basically we learned not to turn our backs on one another and not to trust each other. I'm sure that made us annoyed and resentful, but we never talked about it.

"Later we formed our own little cliques, which we hoped would provide us with support and security. Because we desperately wanted to belong, we were very aggressive about doing almost anything to be acceptable, whatever our group expected of us. We were absolutely petrified that someone would get angry at us, that we would be disliked or cut out of the group. We watched each other like hawks to see if anyone was trying to be better than the rest of us. If so, we started saying bad things about them. Sometimes we banished girls from the group. That happened to me several times. It was a terrible time.

"Looking back I realize we were angry with each other and with ourselves, but we never expressed our feelings through any kind of straightforward aggressive behavior. Rather we were very cagey, secretive, and cruel. We had plenty of role models around, so we were well trained in these bad habits. It's sad that many of us continue to do the same thing as adult women."

By now you may be asking if it is possible to change this dismal picture. Can women candidly face their anger, their aggression? Can they become more capable of dealing with their emotions in ways that will not cause so much pain and destruction?

Margie, a graduate student at Yale, is an example of some-one who is working at addressing those questions. "When I first arrived at my high school in Pittsburgh, I was obsessed with trying to be accepted by my classmates—especially the girls. I tried to cajole them, to compliment them, to ask for help from them, but I was ignored and avoided. I felt very upset, like a total reject. But I knew I couldn't show my feelings.

"About halfway into my second year, I became a part of the 'in group' almost by accident. Franny, one of the girls who didn't like me, was kicked out. So I was invited to join the group as a way of getting back at her. I admit I was happy this happened, but I was also terrified. I knew I had to be very care-ful what I did in order to meet the group's expectations, so I was always under their microscope. I was certain I would do something 'wrong,' and they'd turn their anger on me and kick me out. My mother thought I was going to make myself sick with worry.

"One day another girl, who was not in our group, started talking with me. She was smart and was active in the drama and academic clubs. She wasn't a member of any of the power cliques in our school. What was mind-blowing to me was that she didn't seem to care. We started going for coffee together after school. She invited me to join the drama club.

"It didn't take long before the group got really angry at me for hanging out with her, and they started going after me. They stared at me, mocked me, talked about me, avoided contact with me. They got into huddles whispering and laughing loud-ly and then became silent when I walked up to them. It wasn't easy to prove what they were doing, but they were trying to hurt me without openly attacking me. It really upset me.

"Finally I realized I had had enough; I didn't want to play their games any more. I couldn't do what they did to other girls nor could I allow myself to be destroyed by them. Luckily, I decided to focus more on my studies and other activities. I made friends with several girls who weren't part of any group. It felt great to be free of the constant anxiety of having to be careful what I did. The pain in my stomach started going away and eventually I was able to enjoy myself.

"I wish I could tell other girls and women that they don't need to experience the things my group did to me. They don't have to put up with anger and aggression that are directed at them either. I know it's easy for me to say this now that I'm older, but it's not necessary to be popular with the 'in crowd.' It's much better to be honest with yourself, to find places where you can be yourself, and to express your anger in appropriate ways. Maybe if people realize this, they will feel better about themselves."

Margie is right. Unfortunately it's very difficult for young (or old) women to go against the girls or women who are in power; it feels like swimming against the current. And if you are on your own with little support, it takes lots of courage and strength to do this.

Although we've been told that female anger and aggression *are not* acceptable, we *are* angry and aggressive. Often society rewards us—or at least it doesn't punish us—for concealing these dangerous emotions. But when we try to hide these feelings, we end up inflicting more pain on one another and on ourselves. Perhaps one of the most damaging effects of not facing these feelings openly is that we become dishonest. We might say "Oh, I didn't really mean to hurt someone." Or we try to convince ourselves that we have not been aggressive or that it didn't really matter anyway. Such dishonesty and deceit have a way of breeding loathing and distrust of others and of ourselves. When we betray someone, we are aware that we too can be betrayed. Soon we begin devaluing one another, become disappointed in our relationships, and end up believing the worst about each other. How often we hear women say: "I don't like working with women." "You can't trust another woman." "You have to be careful around women; they're sneaky and dishonest." Eventually we may realize that we are talking about ourselves, that we too are angry, aggressive, and untrustworthy, and our self-worth deteriorates.

But women are proving that it is possible to transform this situation.

Dealing with Anger in Relationships

The primary targets of women's aggression, hostility, violence, and cruelty are other women.
Phyllis Chesler[6]

For too long, the subject of women's anger and aggression has been off limits, almost too "hot" to explore. So we tend to treat these emotions as silent, unacknowledged, unwelcome visitors in our lives and in our relationships. If they happen to rise to the surface, they are stuffed into our already overflowing garbage cans about to explode. It's time to empty those cans. By bringing these feelings out into the open and into the light of day, we may discover how to clean up our acts and to deal with them in new and improved ways. Here's what some courageous women have successfully tried and are suggesting as ideas to help us face and deal with anger in our relationships.

Can you learn how to express your anger appropriately?

Anger that is avoided, ignored, pushed down, or secretly thrown at someone who happens to be nearby is like poison to us and to everyone around us. When I asked Lillian, a very upbeat ninety-two-year-old woman, why she had such a vivacious, positive spirit, she answered, "It's because I've learned how to deal with my anger. It's called self-care." If we can learn how to express our anger constructively, we will defend ourselves against negative energy. Yes, it really is about self-care.

Are you able to avoid personalizing someone's anger?

Sometimes it is difficult to understand the reason for someone's anger or aggressive behavior that *appears* to be directed at us. It's helpful if we can remember that people who are afraid, who feel out of control, or who are helpless often strike out at anyone near them. My neighbor's gentle dog was hit by a car, and she snarled at me as I tried to get near her. I'm certain she would have bitten me, if I had touched her. She was in terrible pain, confused, and angry, and I happened to be in the way of that. If our friends' actions or facial expressions appear angry, we should try not to jump to the conclusion that they are angry at us. They may have been hit by an "emotional car," and we might be in their way.

Are you willing to confront someone who is hurting you?

Sometimes we are so afraid of confrontation that we do anything to avoid it. We may even "allow" people to hurt us. If we can let someone know that their actions are hurting us, that we have feelings, and that we don't want to be ignored or unrecognized, it may help change the situation. Even if it doesn't, we won't feel quite so powerless and ineffective, because we will have spoken up for ourselves. In these conversations, it is helpful if we use "I" statements such as "I feel bad when you . . . " rather than "You did this to me." We may discover that an honest, healthy confrontation is a good way to clear the air.

Can you stay calm around aggression?

When someone responds to anger with more anger, it's like throwing extra fuel on an already hot fire. If someone appears to be angry or seems to act aggressively toward us, it is much better if we can stay calm. First of all, we should never assume that it is our fault; it may not have anything to do with us. Then we need to sort out what is the real source of the person's anger, not what we think it is. And when *we* are angry at someone, it would be useful if we examined what is going on with us. It might not have anything to do with the recipient of our anger either.

Do you know that feeling out of control can cause anger and aggression?

Sometimes it seems that life is completely out of control. We may be overwhelmed trying to balance family responsibilities, relationships, work, finances, or keeping up our homes. In the midst of such chaos, we believe that we are not valued and that our ideas and opinions are not heard. This can cause us to be insecure. We need to be careful. At times like this, we may experience feelings of failure, self-hatred, and rage, and anyone around us can be a target of our frustration.

Are you willing to talk over your feelings?

This is good medicine for all of us. When I'm hurting, I can easily get angry and strike out at whomever is around me. If I talk with someone I trust, who will listen to me without judgment, it feels like the garbage can has been opened and I've dumped out a load of the rotten stuff. Then I feel better. Perhaps we can talk about our feelings of anger to a trusted friend, family member, a counselor, a clergy person, a support group, or to someone we know will not be judgmental. And, if possible, we should try to choose someone who knows our anger isn't directed at them, who understands our need to vent, and who doesn't minimize it. It will relieve the tension and deflate some of the over-the-top aggression.

Do you know when you are practicing indirect aggression?

Sometimes we are in denial that we are being aggressive. It helps if we can examine our behavior and ask ourselves if we are consciously or unconsciously trying to hurt someone by our words, looks, actions, or non-actions. Whenever I'm doing something nasty and ask myself that question, I get a little twinge in my stomach. Then I know it's time to acknowledge what I'm doing and change my behavior. The bottom line: When we "confront" ourselves and do something more appropriate, we will feel relieved and less angry.

Can you take responsibility for causing someone pain?

If we have inflicted our anger or aggression onto someone—whether they deserved it or not—it will be beneficial to admit that to ourselves and to the person we have hurt. It is tremendously healing to acknowledge and own up to our own stuff. Also, we may want to try asking for forgiveness. Our souls will feel lighter and more at peace. That's why religious institutions encourage people to confess their wrongdoings and get things "off their chests."

*Do you know constructive
physical ways to deal with anger?*

Physical activities, like gardening, walking, biking, swimming, or working out are healthy releases, and they offer creative ways to work off anger. If we take time out to do constructive physical activities, we may wonder why we were so angry in the first place. And we might feel a little sheepish if we've already blown our trash all over the place.

*Can you stop self-criticism and
accept others' constructive suggestions?*

Many women are excessively critical of themselves, believing that they are at fault in every difficult situation. Perhaps we, too, are upset with ourselves for anything that seems to go wrong. When people criticize us, we need to listen to their words and carefully sort through whether they are accurate or not. Perhaps we can try to step back to see if there is anything we can learn from this. Sometimes this kind of feedback is better than self-flagellation or lethal self-criticism. By the way, being open to hearing a constructive suggestion is healthier than trying to think of a way to defend ourselves. So we should be learners instead of judgers, and we can stop blaming ourselves.

Do you understand the causes
of your anger and aggression?

When we are able to look candidly at the *causes* of our anger and aggression, we can understand why we have such intense reactions. Sometimes we are angry because we have been deeply hurt, or we have been deprived, attacked, rejected, or treated as unworthy people. Once we comprehend this, we can begin to develop appropriate ways to channel our feelings.

Are you willing to get help, if necessary?

Because of complex events and things that may have happened to us at some time in our lives, our aggression can get out of control. That might not be our fault. But it's really important to acknowledge and understand if our feelings become unmanageable. If so, we may want to reach out for professional assistance. Or if we are the victim of someone's unrestrained anger and aggression, we should try to get help. It is possible for us to have a better quality of life.

If the anger can be addressed without the person feeling she is out of control or damaging the other, it can be useful to both friends.
Luise Eichenbaum and Susie Orbach[7]

WORKING WELL WITH

women

SEVEN

Women enter the job arena with a stronger urge
to form and maintain relationships than men do.
Whether we are talking to the dry cleaner, the
cashier, or the boss, we want to know a life story.
Gail Evans[1]

orking well with women." Whenever I raise
that issue, I receive diverse reactions:

- "Working with women has been wonderful for me. I've developed my best friendships, established networks, and have also found a real safety net."

- "Women can be so hard on themselves. They expect more from each other than they do from men."

- "When a man does something poorly on the job, it's usually acceptable to most women, possibly even great. But if a woman does the same thing, women criticize her for doing it."

- "I don't think women know how to work well with each other."

Not long ago most women in the United States worked only in their homes, and without pay. By 1950, one out of three women in the USA had a paying job. Today more than three out of four women have paying jobs, and nearly 99% of them work for pay at some time in their lives. Although women are the sole earners in two out of every five American families, they only earn about three-quarters of what men earn in similar jobs. In the past twenty years, women have started up nearly 75% of the new businesses in the United States, and 36% of all businesses are owned by women.[2]

With so many women now working, it's important to examine some of the dynamics that take place in the workplace in order to have a clearer understanding of the dilemmas and predicaments that can occur when women work together as colleagues, supervisors, and subordinates. Thus we will be better prepared to face any problems that might arise in the workplace and can develop healthier resolutions.

Let's start with some basic understandings. First, although the words "women working" can include women who care for their homes, raise families, or watch over children and adults, in this chapter "women working" refers to women who work at a paying job in the workplace. Second, it's helpful to remember that for centuries men's rules and systems have set the standard for anyone employed in the working world. In the last decades, more and more women have been entering into what were once thought of as male professions. Since women have only been in the workplace and in leadership roles for a relatively short time, it's too early to predict if major changes will occur in the way they will work together after they have been firmly established as equals and in positions of power for some time.

In an earlier chapter (see "Competition in Friendship"), we acknowledged that many women have problems coping with competition of any type. But whether we like it or not, the workplace, under male or female supervision, is loaded with competition. This is due to limited resources, positions, and funds, as well as the nature of human beings' interactions with one another. Because of their aversion to competition in general, many women experience competition in the workplace— whether it is visible or hidden—as frightening and treacherous.

This seems to be especially true in professions dominated by men.

Women who work in highly competitive, male-dominated environments face a number of challenges. Mandy, a forty-eight-year-old human resources director in a large corporation in Houston, Texas, describes some of them. "Men and women have very dissimilar styles of behavior, so women often have problems working in what I call 'a man's world.' We usually think of women's behavior as nurturing, sensitive, people-oriented, receptive, and encouraging. On the other hand, men's behavior is often defined as aggressive, controlling, competitive, decisive, forceful, or authoritative. Clearly these are two very different types of behavior. Therefore, it's challenging to find a common ground, and many women find it difficult to adapt to a work environment that is run by men and men's rules."

So it is not a surprise that women have a tough time discovering an acceptable way to behave on the job that is not viewed as too masculine or too feminine. If a woman works in a traditionally supportive, feminine way in a male-dominated workplace, she may be judged as too soft or too weak, not tough enough to be successful or promoted. If she acts in a more masculine way, she is criticized by both men and women as being too competitive, aggressive, and intense. In order to be successful in organizations where there are very few females at the top, some women feel forced to take actions that might not be considered ethical or professional in order to get ahead, such as trying to hold back other women from succeeding.

Brenda, a thirty-seven-year-old attorney in New York City, describes an unpleasant situation at her law firm that has only three female senior partners. "The women who have made it as partners are very competitive and not at all accessible to those of us who are junior to them. What is worse is the way they flirt or act overly deferential around the male partners in the office. It's demoralizing for the younger women. It's common knowledge that one of the female partners slept her way to the top. I admit I don't feel comfortable around these women."

In contrast, research shows that in work situations where many women are in high positions, women who are subordinates will experience more support and mentoring from female managers than where there are few women at the top. Patty works in a law firm in Baltimore where there are almost as many women in senior positions as men. Her story sounds quite different from Brenda's. "I really appreciate the female partners in my firm. They are supportive to the junior women, and there is a healthy spirit of cooperation. One of the partners has become my mentor, and she helps me whenever I have a problem. She doesn't appear to be jealous or resentful when someone compliments my work. I honestly believe she wants me to be promoted."

When talking about work situations, many women bring up the subject of working for a female "boss." Some women say they prefer working for women because they share information, are more sensitive, supportive, and good team players. Helene, a twenty-eight-year-old junior manager in a department store in Delaware, told me about her female boss. "She is kind, patient, smart—*very* smart, and caring. She's always open to hearing new ideas. But she's also firm and knows where to draw the line of her boundaries. Although she is friendly, I don't think of her as 'my friend.' She has a clear vision where her department is headed, and she gets her staff to work together as a team. I believe she is respected and trusted by almost everyone. I enjoy working with her."

Other women say they don't like to work for a female boss, that women in power positions are too competitive, demanding, authoritative, controlling, and bossy. Georgia, a forty-year-old factory worker in Rhode Island, said, "My supervisor works her employees as if she is the Gestapo. She is mean and manipulative, and she frightens everyone. She keeps the women at odds with each other, talks about them to other employees, and encourages backstabbing and gossip. Everyone seems to be suspicious of each other. It's a terrible way to work."

After listening to a number of women talk about their supervisors, I came to the conclusion that male and female bosses really aren't much different from each other: They can be good, mediocre, bad, terrible. Occasionally problems occur because women have expectations of female supervisors that are not realistic; they assume that a woman will be more sympathetic toward them or will behave in ways that are more principled than men. If those expectations are not met, they feel disappointed and let down.

Often women are envious of the success of their female colleagues, as was the case of my friend Betty (see "Rising above Envy"). After she became the head of a large corporation, she learned that the female employees and her friends were gossiping that she was acting "just like a man." Eventually they stopped supporting her and started attacking her.

Women who have not had healthy relationships with their mothers are often intimidated by a female supervisor at work. Or they have difficulty trusting a woman who is more capable or experienced than they are. Some women are not open to working with women at all, so they try to put a female supervisor "in her place" by talking about her, using threats, humiliation, and accusations—direct and indirect. Phyllis Chesler points out that an unacknowledged tension in the workplace is that women may have an "unconscious desire to be protected by a Fairy Godmother, coupled with her unconscious fear that an Evil Stepmother will emerge instead. Thus, women's expectations of each other at work are often unrealistic, sexist, and characterized by unspoken ambivalence, regardless of who objectively holds more power."[3]

When a woman supervisor has high standards and expectations of her employees or doesn't treat them in nurturing or encouraging ways, she may be seen as heartless or unfeeling. Most likely she will be disliked, even feared. Dana was a fifty-two-year-old administrator of a non-profit organization in Missouri. "When I started working there, I saw how poorly things were managed. I thought it was time to make the organization more professional, a place where people would be proud to work. But I had enormous problems with the female employees. They didn't want me to make any changes. They told me that I was callous and cold-blooded, that I was trying to make women work like men. Just who did I think I was? It felt like they were out to destroy me. Eventually, they got to me and I decided to leave the organization."

In her book *Feminine Leadership*, Marilyn Loden highlights the inconsistent ways that people view men and women at work. Her humorous but rather honest listing of the differences between a businessman and a businesswoman include:

- A businessman is aggressive; a businesswoman is pushy.

- A businessman is good on details; she's picky.

- He loses his temper at times because he's so involved in his work; she's bitchy.

- He knows how to follow through; she doesn't know when to quit.

- He stands firm; she's hard.

- He is a man of the world; she's been around.

- He isn't afraid to say what he thinks; she's mouthy.

- He's a stern taskmaster; she's hard to work for.[4]

Another rather common problem is that women tend to be overly emotional about their work. Often they take criticism or suggestions too personally (see "Recognizing Needs and Feelings"). They may be extremely needy, overly sensitive, and excitable. "For years, I've supervised dozens of male and female clerical workers. I have to admit it's the female employees who usually give me trouble," says Penny, a fifty-five-year-old supervisor in a New Mexico business. "You never know what's going on with them. They are thin-skinned, touchy, and loaded with a lot of emotional stuff, and they are easily upset or get their feelings hurt. Some women become hysterical if I give them directions to improve their work; they think I'm criticizing or punishing them. They want me to be sympathetic, supportive, and accommodating. They tell me that since I'm a woman, I should know what they're going through and be more understanding and nicer to them. It's like I'm supposed to be their mother just because we happen to share the same gender. But I won't play Mommy for them."

Many women find it difficult to work in heavily male-dominated workplaces, because they have to endure circumstances that seem unbearable and out of their control. It makes them feel inadequate. Some women try to locate a work setting that is either run by women or is more female-oriented. Others attempt to start their own businesses. Sometimes that is an improvement, and the work place is more comfortable and supportive for them. But that's not always the case.

A number of studies point out that women who work in female-managed workplaces may mistakenly view their work settings as being more nurturing and family oriented. As a result, they have difficulty directly communicating their feelings about problems and are cautious about any kind of open conflict. They may be afraid to challenge or confront the "mother boss." In such an environment, workers can easily become petty, gossipy, and backstabbing.

Rosalie, a bubbly twenty-six-year-old mother from Atlanta, talked with enthusiasm about her workplace. "I work in a small women's business, where there's no competition. We're a big family all taking care of each other. Our owner is like a mother to us. She lets us work part-time and have flexible hours. She's especially open to young mothers working for her." That sounds impressive, but perhaps somewhat unrealistic. When I spoke with another woman in this "non-competitive" business, her comments were quite different from Rosalie's. "The owner hires young mothers to work for her on a part-time, flexible basis so she doesn't have to pay their benefits. She takes advantage of them. Because they are afraid they might lose their jobs, they won't challenge, disagree, or oppose anything she says or does. I believe they want their workplace to be like a happy family and their boss to be what they hoped their own mothers would be for them. Unfortunately that's just not possible."

During my lifetime, most of my experiences working with women have been very positive. I've been supported by brilliant women who mentored me and challenged me to grow, and I've been promoted by strong women who helped me to move ahead. I have also had work situations with women that weren't very positive. In fact, a few of them have been down-right miserable. I was fired by a not-very-competent woman manager who had less experience and background than I did in our field. Another female supervisor told me that I did my job "too well and too fast" and, therefore, was a threat to the other staff. And a female colleague, who was also my friend, whom I thought I could trust with my life, completely tore me to shreds behind my back. So I know what it feels like to be the target of women's envy, competition, anger, and aggression in the workplace.

Looking back, I recognize that I've learned a lot from these challenging experiences. And if they occurred today, I doubt that I'd allow them to happen in the same way or that they would have such an impact on me. For example, what once seemed to be one of my most dreadful "working-with-women" stories now makes me laugh. But at the time it didn't seem very funny. I was a third grade teacher in Florida, and I loved my work. Teaching kids at that level is a natural high; they're full of energy and optimism, and they honestly like to learn. Most teachers in the elementary grades seem to enjoy helping students grow and mature. Working with people who share a common mission makes it easy to form strong relationships.

In my school there were three third-grade teachers, and we were asked to produce the school play that year. As a go-getter, I immediately began to plan how we could work on costumes, scenery, music, rehearsals. I was committed to doing whatever was needed—from putting music together, rehearsing the chorus, working on scenery and costumes, to helping students learn their lines. Ingrid, one of my two colleagues was right there with me, but Darlene, the third teacher, said she wasn't feeling well, so she couldn't help with the production. And she didn't—not one bit.

The night of the performance, the kids were great. They knew *most* of their lines, sang like angels, and didn't go completely wild when the lights went out. By the time the play was over, the audience was impressed, and I was elated as I helped move scenery, directed the chorus, and played the piano. I was running a slight temperature from a bad cold, so I was hot and clammy. But it didn't matter, because the performance couldn't have gone better. While I pounded away on the piano sweating profusely, pride filled my heart as the curtain was opened for a second curtain call. I was shocked when I saw Darlene step out of the wings onto the stage in front of the lights. Not one drop of sweat marred her impeccably made up face, and she didn't look tired or sick. In fact, she looked absolutely radiant. She smiled at the audience and took a deep bow as they exuberantly applauded. And if that wasn't enough, someone came to the stage and handed Darlene a bouquet of flowers. I confess there wasn't a single kind thought in my heart!

Despite the fact that there are many stories about the difficulties women have with working together, there are also many stories about women who work well with each other. A large corporation in the Midwest tested the theory that people—especially women—who work together as a supportive team are more successful on the job than if they would be in cutthroat competition with each other. My friend Ella talks about her experience: "Our group was led by a strong, compassionate woman manager who had clear boundaries, high expectations, and a great sense of humor. She treated all of us as experts, and our talents were honored and celebrated. There was no place for petty or negative chitchat about each other or our management; it simply wasn't part of our culture. Since we were expected to cooperate, there was very little aggression or envy among the staff. We had access to lots of information, which we shared freely with each other because we were not in competition with each other. Everyone was encouraged to bring new ideas and possible solutions to any challenges or problems we faced. In this atmosphere, we felt empowered and were free to appreciate each other's accomplishments and successes.

"During those years I thoroughly enjoyed working with our team. Many of my female colleagues became my dear friends. It was the ideal working situation for me. So it was really sad when the leadership and culture at our corporation changed. My manager retired, and now people have to compete for the few jobs available. Fortunately I'm still friends with the women who worked on my team. In fact, they are now my personal support group even though we no longer work together. Our friendships have endured more than twenty years."

And there's another hope-filled story. The Union Center for Women in Brooklyn, New York, has been a special gift to me and many other women. Over thirty years ago, I had a dream that if women were given a supportive, encouraging environment where they were appreciated and respected, they could easily work together without toxic competition and envy. I believed it was actually their natural mode of operation. I also trusted that in such an atmosphere women would be compassionate and caring to each other without being overly aggressive, catty, or gossipy. My dream came true when a group of women and I created the Union Center for Women as a non-profit organization.

Through the years, the overall mission of the Center has continued to be the same: to provide women a place of support where they can learn to work together without the usual problems of destructive rivalry, vicious envy, and harsh criticism found in many competitive workplaces. At the center, women try out new possibilities for themselves, develop their potential, learn who they really are, and encourage each other to grow. Over the years, thousands of women have participated in, supported, and managed the Union Center for Women. Today, over three decades later, the Center is still in operation. It has gone through many transformations and leadership changes, but the basic premise still holds: When given the opportunity in an appropriate setting, women can and do work well together.

Working Well with Women

• •

Other women say that they prefer working for women—they are good listeners, they're smart, they share information, they're supportive, they're good team players.

BJ Gallagher[5]

Since almost every one of us will work with women at a paying job at some time in our lives, we want to make our experiences with each other as positive as possible. Here are ideas that some resourceful women developed that have strengthened their ability to work well with women.

Do you have realistic expectations about female relationships at work?

Women colleagues in the workplace are not our sisters or our best friends—nor are they our enemies. They are simply our colleagues. Our expectations in the workplace should be about doing a job well, being professional, and being treated fairly. It's not reasonable to expect a woman at work to be our supporter or to act like a close family member. When we see women in the workplace realistically and non-idealistically for who and what they really are, we will do a better job, and we won't be disappointed by the outcome.

Can you stop worrying about what people say about you?

Because women are relatively new in the workplace, it will take some time before people are totally accustomed to our being there. If we are good workers or strong managers, we likely are self-assured, assertive, and perhaps forceful. However, some people might think of us as overly aggressive, hard-hitting, and cold. That's just the way it is. If we want to do an excellent job or move ahead, we might as well get used to this. We don't need to lower our standards at work, and we should always be fair, open, positive, and competent. Perhaps someday people will appreciate us and our work.

Do you network and collaborate in a team approach?

Research studies have confirmed that people working in team approaches accomplish more than those who work only as individuals. In a study by Alfie Kohn, he points out that people don't perform better when they are trying "to beat others"; rather, they are more successful at carrying out their goals when they work together.[6] Some innovative companies reward people for cooperating, for supporting each other's creative ideas, and for working well together. Since women are superb teachers and know how to nurture relationships, we may want to cultivate positive relationships, networks, and teamwork at our workplaces. Perhaps our teams will create something beautiful together.

Is it possible to not be overly emotional at work?

When we were little girls, we cried or ran to our parents for sympathy if we thought someone hurt us or if someone looked at us the wrong way. Many women still act like children when a supervisor or colleague says something negative about their work. Or they become overly emotional about difficult situations in the workplace. If we are to be taken seriously, we have to have tougher skins and not take everything as a personal attack or an unfair decision. We will be respected more when we act professionally.

Do you see yourself as powerless?

It has often been said that we are as good as our own self-image. So how we see ourselves in the workplace will have a lot to do with how we perform. If we see ourselves as weak, helpless, and ineffective, we will likely perform that way and be treated that way. What's worse, our colleagues and supervisors will not value us. We need to accept that each of us is capable, effective, and talented. And if our skills that are required to do our jobs are weak, then we should consider sharpening them up through study, training, mentors, or whatever it takes.

Can you set limits and establish boundaries?

Women are accustomed to having almost no boundaries, and they are all-too-familiar with having people infringe on their privacy and their space at home and at work (see "The Plus of Boundaries"). So it may be difficult for us to set limits and stick to them. Unless we really enjoy being martyrs and like people dumping things on our desks, we need to learn to say "no" and ask people to respect the limits of our job description. If we don't, we will be saddled with someone else's responsibilities and end up working far too many hours. We have to recognize that *we ourselves* have the power to *not* allow ourselves to feel frustrated and over-used.

Do you treat yourself and other women with respect?

When women compete in the workplace, they tend to be their own worst enemies. Women can be tough on one another and often hurt each other more than men do. One positive way to change the way things happen in the workplace is to treat other women—and ourselves—with dignity and respect. It's essential to keep in mind the importance of valuing other women, because *we* are one of them too. Perhaps other women will follow our examples and do the same.

Are you capable of using your
best female assets in a positive way?

We may be surprised at how many wonderful skills women have that are excellent qualities in the workplace. These include being good listeners, being cooperative, nurturing relationships, being understanding and considerate. When we acknowledge our best female resources and maximize them, we can use them in a positive way in the workplace.

Can you avoid conforming to negative female stereotypes?

We have all seen or heard about numerous negative images of women in the workplace, including their acting weak and powerless, being too emotional, backstabbing other women, not having any boundaries or limits, flirting with men in order to get ahead, and sleeping their way to the top. If we conform to any of these stereotypes, it will be detrimental for us in the workplace. More importantly, it will lower our self-image and make us feel disappointed in ourselves.

Do you know how to keep a sense of humor?

In the workplace, there are many very angry and frustrated people. But work doesn't really deserve such enormous negative emotional responses; it should be something we enjoy, at least part of the time. Appropriate humor can put things in perspective, level things out, and take the sting out of highly aggressive competition or conflicts. But we have to recognize that humor should only be used at the right times and with a sense of style.

If you are burned by a woman
in the workplace, do you give up?

Just because we have encountered incompetent, envious, or passive-aggressive female colleagues or supervisors doesn't mean that every interaction with women in the workplace has to be unpleasant. Certainly it's beneficial if we are able to be alert, somewhat guarded, and can read the caution signs carefully. But we may be pleasantly surprised to discover that there are wonderful, competent, fair, supportive women working with us. Probably they are not that different from us—or from men either. So we will be open to the possibilities.

- -

No matter how apparently successful someone becomes, she still needs her friends. . . . What is success if we can't share it with our girlfriends?

Carmen Renee Berry and Tamara Traeder[7]

THE PLUS OF

boundaries

The number one problem for women ... is saying no. Sad, because it is such a positive and freeing word.

Judith Selee McClure[1]

When I was growing up on the farm in Nebraska, my dad told me that we needed to have fences with gates, not solid walls, around our farm. By staking out the boundaries of our property, it was clear where our property began and ended, what was ours and therefore was our responsibility. Boundaries also showed us what was not ours, so we knew what was not our responsibility. Having boundaries provided protection for our property, kept animals from roaming in and out of our land, and gave us a sense of security. They also allowed us, as well as others, to enter and exit as necessary. The same supposition also applies for people—especially women. With clearly defined boundaries—not walls—we can protect our "property" and not allow bad things to happen. We can keep out the people, activities, and demands that may be harmful to us. We can invite what we want or need into our lives, and we can open and close the gates to our property as necessary. Having boundaries allows us to take responsibility for our own lives, protects us, and gives us a sense of freedom.

But without clear boundaries we do not know where we "end" or someone else "begins," and we spend time worrying, spinning our wheels, doing things we shouldn't, and using up a lot of extra energy. Without boundaries, options and possibilities become more limited for us. What's worse, we may not be able to choose what we need or want to do with our lives, and we may discover that we have turned ourselves into prisoners—without any fences or walls.

Many women find it difficult to set and honor boundaries for themselves and for others. They seem to forget that each person is a unique and separate being who should be responsible for her own life. Being responsible means letting others know what we require or want, what we like or dislike, what we will allow or not allow—in other words, setting limits. And, of course, we need to learn to respect the boundaries of others.

Women whose boundaries are weak have a problem saying no to the pressures, demands, needs, and control of others. They fear that if they refuse to give in to the requests of others or say no, that the relationship may be jeopardized or they will not be liked. Although some women take on almost any request that comes their way, they may inwardly resent this and end up feeling angry, frustrated, and resentful. Usually the pressure to do this does not come from an outside source, but rather from an internal obligation—"I should" do something. Henry Cloud and John Townsend write that people "give in repeatedly to some irresponsible or demanding person. Then, out of the blue, they'll pack up and leave the relationship with no warning."[2]

Molly, a thirty-five-year-old stay-at-home mom in Cape Cod, has a difficult time defining her needs and expressing what are her limits to others and to herself. She explains her situation this way. "I am so overextended with responsibilities related to my family, my church, my kids' schools, and other volunteer activities. My biggest problem is that I'm too busy; I don't have enough time for everything. My family complains that I'm not with them enough, I don't see my friends, and I don't have time to do some of the things I'd really like to do. But when someone says, 'You are such a good worker, would you mind doing this one favor?' or 'I really need your help,' I can't seem to tell them no. So I end up agreeing to their request. Perhaps they would be offended if I turned them down or they might never ask me to do something again. I'm sure it's not good to be stretched this thin. But I like being asked to do things, to have the feeling that I am needed by someone. So I'll probably continue doing this. It's in my nature."

It seems that Molly has lost control over her life. Although she says she likes the feeling of being needed, she may not really enjoy that her own "property" is not protected. Like many other women, she suffers from an overwhelming need to be accepted and liked. So when someone manipulates her into giving more than she really can, she does it. But the price is high, and Molly could end up being burned out, feeling unappreciated, losing friends, and missing something she really wanted.

Many women respond to the requests and demands of others because they believe they are powerless and thus unable to choose how they should react. Some want to appear competent, dynamic, worthy, and energetic. Others feel incapable of taking responsibility for their choices. They deny that they have made a decision or they lay the responsibility for their decisions on others. Therefore, someone else is to blame for whatever happens. I had a classmate in college who felt she had no control over any decision making. "I didn't really want to do that," she lamented, "but my boyfriend made me do it." And "I'm studying to be a teacher, because that's what my folks want me to do."

Another serious boundary issue for women is the need to please, which may grow out of their fear of being alone. Some women believe, "If I do enough, people won't leave me." Women who constantly try to please do not necessarily respond to other peoples' requests out of their own free will or because they have a big heart. Most likely, they yearn for acceptance and love, so they unconsciously try to please people. Harriet B. Braiker writes in her book *The Disease to Please*: "People-pleasing is driven by a fixed thought that you need and must strive for *everyone* to like you. You measure your self-esteem and define your identity by how much you do for others whose needs, you insist, *must* come before your own . . . you believe that being *nice* will protect you from rejection and other hurtful treatment from others."[3] According to Braiker, there are numerous pressures related to the obligations of being a people-pleaser. Here is what she calls the "shoulds" in "The Ten Commandments of People-Pleasing":

1. I should always do what others want, expect, or need from me.
2. I should take care of everyone around me whether they ask for help or not.
3. I should always listen to everyone's problems and try my best to solve them.
4. I should always be nice and never hurt anyone's feelings.
5. I should always put other people first, before me.
6. I should never say no to anyone who needs or requests something of me.
7. I should never disappoint anyone or let others down in any way.
8. I should always be happy and upbeat and never show any negative feelings to others.
9. I should always try to please other people and make them happy.
10. I should try never to burden others with my own needs or problems.[4]

Allison, a thirty-eight-year-old librarian in Concord, New Hampshire, is an example of a people-pleaser. She's a perfectionist and extremely demanding of herself, especially when it comes to doing something for others. She almost never says no to a request for help, and she tends to do too much. When she agrees to take on an enormous task, she doesn't ask for help or delegate parts of the assignment to others. "As an only child growing up in a suburban area, I often felt lonely and isolated. My parents were successful business people who worked long hours and didn't have a lot of time or patience for me. I don't remember them telling me that I did anything well. I was always afraid that I would do something wrong, that I would disappoint them or make them angry, and they might not love me. So I'm grateful whenever someone trusts me, needs me, or thinks I can do something well for them.

"Last week a woman from my club told me she heard that I was very responsible, that I never did a job half way. She knew I was the right person to head up a very important project, and it would please her if I would do it. I admit it felt great when she said that, so without hesitating I told her I would, even though I wasn't sure how I would find the time, and I knew my husband would be upset with me. Yes, I'm involved in many activities, and my marriage and close friendships are sometimes neglected because of my hectic schedule. But when someone asks me to do something for them, I can't say 'no.' I don't want to let them down, and I'm certain they will like what I do."

Allison may not realize that she is suffering from the addiction of pleasing people. Like other addictions, hers is driven by fears of rejection, criticism, and abandonment. As is true for many women, Allison's self-esteem is tied up with how much she can do for others and how successful she is at pleasing them. By fulfilling other peoples' needs, Allison believes she will gain love and self-worth. It's as though she were taking out an insurance policy against the risks of disapproval and desertion.

Many people-pleasers have hidden expectations concerning how people, who make demands of them, should respond back to them. They expect that people will appreciate, like, or approve of them for what they have done; and that these people in turn will not criticize, reject, abandon, or treat them unfairly. But since these assumptions are not articulated or made clear, other people do not have a clue about them and thus are unable to meet them. So a people-pleaser may wind up feeling disappointed or resentful toward the people she wanted to please. Furthermore, she will not be able to express those feelings since that would be going against the unspoken commandment of never showing that she is disappointed or frustrated. Because women are so accustomed to having their boundaries violated, they often replicate this unsound way of relating to others. Without realizing what they are doing, they make the same unrealistic and controlling demands of others—especially of women.

There's yet another important aspect to consider in this dilemma. Becoming a martyr or victim is not a good way to make or keep friends. For people who are boundary-less, this is a difficult concept to grasp. Most people do not appreciate someone who is self-sacrificing or overly generous. A woman who does everything for everyone and endlessly gives of herself to family, friends, colleagues, even strangers, can make others feel guilty and reluctantly indebted to her, especially if she does not allow them to give something back. As a giver who doesn't receive, she denies others the enjoyment and satisfaction of giving. She could easily be viewed as a manipulative and controlling person, which may be what she is. Even if a woman is acting out of her best intentions, people who are on the receiving end may get angry and resentful because they feel they have been pushed into a situation of indebtedness that may not be comfortable for them.

Often the issue of boundaries and control comes up in the workplace (see "Working Well with Women"). Women who need to please or be liked by their supervisors are unable to say no to demands made of them. I confess that I'm a "recovering boundary-less woman." After some bad experiences, I've learned that saying yes and being open to doing everything for everyone doesn't automatically earn approval, respect, appreciation, or security on the job. When I was working at an international non-profit organization, I was the manager of a large department. I did my job well and had excellent results, but I worked hard and put in very long hours. At the time it didn't really bother me, because I enjoyed the work and was dedicated to it. So I willingly took on extra projects that my supervisor and staff asked me to do. One day my supervisor called me into his office and informed me that he was transfer-ring half of my administrative staff to another department in the organization. I was shocked when he told me the reason: The other department wasn't doing well, and they needed strong staff. When I replied that I couldn't possibly get the work done without them, he laughed. "You probably would get the work done—and done well—even if I moved every one of the support staff out of your department."

It took that kind of outrageous wake-up call before I understood what I was doing to myself. Since I had so firmly established my working style, I realized that I needed to leave and go to another workplace where I could start over again. Although establishing boundaries and not trying to please everyone has been an ongoing battle for me, I've made a lot of progress. And I'm far less frustrated and not so exhausted.

Karen, a fifty-four-year-old veterinarian who owns her own business in Charlottesville, Virginia, talked about her struggle with boundaries. "For years, I had a really hard time delegat-ing. I think it was partly because I got a lot of ego strokes from being able to do everything myself. I needed to believe that I could do most of the work without much support. I con-vinced myself that no one else would be able to do what I could do or do it as well. One day I realized that I was running out of gas. I felt stressed out and absolutely depleted, and my physical and emotional health were suffering.

"Shortly after that, I learned how contagious and debilitat-ing stress can be. It not only did damage to my well-being, but it started affecting my staff, my family, and my friends. I always thought of myself as Ms. Nice, but I was turning into a shriek-ing, short-tempered, angry woman.

"One day I realized that most of my staff resented me and they certainly didn't feel a sense of loyalty to me. One woman blew up and accused me of trying to micromanage everyone and everything. It dawned on me that my unwillingness to del-egate, because I thought nobody would do the work as well as I could, was only part of the story. What was going on was my need to control everything. But by being so controlling, I not only hurt myself and my business, but I also prevented my staff from growing and learning. They weren't developing their skills, and I was cheating them from feeling a sense of accomplishment.

"At first I thought I should give up my business and just work for another veterinarian. But then I decided to try delegating some of the assignments to others and let go of my tightly held reins. I realized things didn't have to be perfect. I was astounded at how quickly and positively the staff responded and how much better the work went. And I felt good too. I learned that my value as a person does not depend on what I do or my being able to control everything." Karen ended her story with some good advice for others who might want to settle their own boundary and control issues: "I'd like to suggest to women who have boundary or control problems that they ask themselves some really hard questions about why they are doing everything, why they have no boundaries, why they need to be so controlling. They might be surprised at their answers, and they may discover that there are better, more enjoyable, and more effective ways to gets things done."

So if you don't have well-defined boundaries, or you are a people-pleaser, or you try to control everything, you may want to learn how to avoid being exhausted, overextended, and exploited. After all, it is difficult saying yes to everyone and then trying to stay tuned to their needs and wishes. Although you may be successful at pleasing some people, your conscious and unconscious fears of being rejected, abandoned, or of not being liked probably will not go away. In fact they may increase. If you continue to try to control everything or you overextend yourself, you may find yourself feeling angry, disappointed, frustrated, and unhappy. Before you get to that point, or if you're already there, it's time to think about some other strategies.

Experiencing the Plus of Boundaries

* *

By allowing others to repay your kindnesses and reciprocate your giving, you will be doing a bigger favor for others than by leaving them beholden or in your debt.

Harriet B. Braiker[5]

As Karen suggests, there are better, more enjoyable, and more effective ways to get things done than by being a boundary-less person. Here's what women with healthy boundaries have suggested as possible ideas to help us free ourselves of some of those tricky and awkward boundary issues so we can experience the advantages of boundaries.

Do you know and accept who you are and what your limits are?

Many boundary-less women search endlessly for their acceptance and approval from others because they feel unworthy and unlovable. Knowing and accepting ourselves are important ingredients in establishing boundaries. This knowledge starts by recognizing what *our* reality is, and what *our* truth is. It also includes understanding who and what we are or can be, what we can and cannot do, and what we do and do not want to do. Once we are aware of that, we will understand where our limits and our boundaries should be set—physically, emotionally, and spiritually. Then, our lives will not be so scattered and chaotic, and we will have a sense of integrity and honesty about ourselves. It's useful if we can keep in mind that we don't really need other people's approval to have a fulfilling and meaningful life. But we do need our own. So we might want to think about how we can appreciate ourselves and live our lives fully.

Are you able to establish boundaries?

As women, we are accustomed to having few or no boundaries. People often infringe on our privacy or our space at home or at work, so it's difficult for us to set limits and stick to them. Remember: When the frontier was settled, the first thing the pioneers did was stake out their property. Otherwise, their land would have been overrun, pilfered, embezzled, stampeded, and part of the public domain. That's not a place we want our lives to be. So unless we really enjoy having people dump things on us (if we do, we may want to take a hard look at that), we should try to stake out our property and establish our own boundaries.

Do you tell people what your boundaries are?

Women can be spineless and rather pathetic about letting people know where their boundaries begin and end. So out of a lack of awareness, people continue to take advantage of them and steal their stuff. Some women get upset believing they can't do anything about this problem. But in reality they—and we—can. So if we don't want to get stuck with someone else's responsibilities and feel used or resentful, we need to tell people what our limitations are. Most people will appreciate our saying, "I would like to help you, but I realize that I'm already stretched too thin" or, "I need to pay more attention to my health/work/family." It will save us from saying something we really shouldn't, from the embarrassment of blowing up at someone, and from doing permanent damage to what might have been a good relationship. People will respect us more and our lives will be less complicated.

Are you able to say "no"?

It isn't useful to say "yes" unwillingly because we feel forced or manipulated into doing something. Indeed, a reluctant "yes" might really be a controlling mechanism. If we don't have the time, energy, resources, or the desire to do something, it's better to say a firm "no." That little word informs people that we are in charge of our lives, we have clear boundaries, and we have an existence that is separate from them. We especially need suitable boundaries at our workplace. We might try meeting with our group or with management to set priorities. By doing this, we may relieve ourselves of burdens that we shouldn't be encumbered with in the first place. The word "no" does not make us unlikable, nor does the word "yes" make us acceptable, desired after, or endearing. We can be women who say "yes" and "no" as appropriate.

Do you see yourself as having power in your own right?

A woman's self-image can determine how she will be treated by others. If we see ourselves as weak, helpless, and ineffective, we will likely act and be treated that way, and our boundaries will not protect us. Therefore colleagues, supervisors, friends, and family members can easily take advantage of our states of mind. Start imagining who and what we can be: capable, effective, strong, talented, and valuable. That small step alone will help launch us into settling some of our boundary and control issues.

Can you allow others to give something back to you?

One of the nicest things we can do is permit others to give us something, whatever that might be. When I worked in Pakistan, a poor, but wise woman in one of the slums of Karachi told me, "You're very good at giving us things we need—maybe too good. But when you do this, you take away some of our respect and dignity. It would be better if you would let us give something back to you, no matter how big or small. It would be a kind thing to do." This is a very important lesson for all of us to learn.

Do you take good care of yourself and take time off?

People who are not willing to take time off or to care for themselves may be headed for a crisis. Taking a break from a project, an organization, demanding relationships, and family issues can provide new perspectives and possible solutions to problems. In the Scriptures, Jesus told people to love their neighbors as *they love themselves*. It's almost impossible to love or care for our neighbors in a sincere and helpful way if we do not love and care for ourselves. So if we are women who always take care of other peoples' problems and needs rather than minding our own, we might discover one day that we are exhausted, burned out, and unable to help anyone. The Red Cross reminds us that we can't give blood if we're anemic. This is good advice.

Can you remove yourself from high-risk situations?

If it is clear to us that we are in danger of overextending ourselves, we may need to remove ourselves at least temporarily from a situation. From a distance we may be able to see the bigger picture and get a better perspective. Also, this action may clarify for ourselves and others the need for boundaries that are honored and respected.

Do you recognize that you have choices?

Although some women who are boundary-less believe they don't really have choices, in reality everyone has some kind of choice. Even deciding not to choose is a choice. We may want to start making some healthy choices for ourselves, like not spending time with people who are negative. So let's choose to make good choices and surround ourselves with supportive, positive people who respect boundaries—ours and theirs, too.

Can you inform people that you, too, have needs and problems?

If we don't let people know that we have our own set of needs, we are in for some demanding and difficult times. It's better if we inform people, who *need* to know, that we have concerns or problems and that we would appreciate their help. Most people—just like us—want to be helpful, and they want to be appreciated when they do lend a hand.

Are you able to build a support network and get help?

Some women put up with all kinds of things, including abuse, because they do not feel worthy or they are afraid they will be unwanted if they stand up to someone. If we are being abused by someone but are concerned that setting boundaries will cause us to be abandoned or not loved, we may need to seek professional assistance or join a support group. Being in a supportive environment may give us the strength to say "no" to abusive situations and help us create boundaries for ourselves.

• •

Boundaries define us. They define what is me and what is not me. A boundary shows me where I end and someone else begins, leading me to a sense of ownership.

Henry Cloud and John Townsend[6]

MEN AND

friendships

NINE

To get a husband—or, at least, a steady sweetheart—becomes a more and more urgent business. This concern is often destructive of feminine friendships.

Simone de Beauvoir[1]

When I was a little girl growing up on a Nebraska farm, the whole world seemed open to me. As I roamed freely on our land, I felt all-powerful and invincible. I was confident that when I grew up I could be whatever I wanted to be. After reading books about Babe Ruth and Lou Gehrig of the New York Yankees, I was so impressed by these legendary men that I decided that I would grow up to be a baseball player—for the Yankees, of course. For a while, people smiled kindly and patted me on the head when I told them about my dream. But one day, a neighboring farmer put me in my place. "You can't ever be a Yankee," he snickered. "After all, you're only a girl. I sure hope when you grow up you'll be able to find a man who will be a good husband." On a gloomy day in Nebraska, that farmer burst my bubble when he gave me the heartbreaking news: As a girl, I was inferior to boys and therefore unable to compete with them. Furthermore, I would be downright lucky if I could find myself a decent husband. My fantasy of being someone significant and powerful was abruptly and thoughtlessly shattered.

So how could this have happened to me—and to countless other little girls? Let's take a look at some of the forces at work that have the capacity to fracture the hopes and dreams of young girls. Throughout early childhood, most girls feel free, independent, and sovereign. The possibilities available to them seem unlimited and unrestricted. They are not afraid to say what they want, they can excel in their schoolwork, they can easily join boys in games. The future feels wide open for little girls, and they can dream of becoming anything they want to be. But then this bright, bigger-than-life picture for girls can change to one that is narrow and limiting.

For centuries, societal norms and customs have caused the female sex to accept, mostly unconsciously, that they are less important and less valuable than men. Many girls and women are unaware and possibly unable to comprehend the effects on their lives of biases and prejudices that have been stacked against them over time. According to Simone de Beauvoir, a girl is "habituated to seeing in him (the male) a superb being whom she cannot possibly equal. . . . There is no other way out for her than to lose herself, body and soul, in him who is represented to her as the absolute, as the essential."[2]

Undoubtedly girls' future interactions and relations with men are based on their earliest relationships with their fathers. To most young girls, their fathers are bigger-than-life with amazing, almost magical, powers. Later as adults, they unconsciously look for the same security and peace they remember having experienced in their earliest days with their dads. So when they hear a man tell them "you are my baby" or "my little girl," it sounds like music to their ears. Being children again in men's safe arms can fill them with a sense of bliss and comfort. As they grow up, some girls imagine themselves being male or in a male role, so they too can feel superior. But when they are finally forced to realize that it is not possible for them to be as powerful or influential as a man, as I did when I was told I couldn't be a Yankee, they are no longer able to remain in that fantasy. Sometimes they try to share male influence and clout by getting a man to fall in love with them. Even when they want to choose the route of being independent, having a man still seems easier and more attractive for the majority of women. After all, society's compelling message to women is that they don't need to fight their way through the complicated world on their own; rather they can choose to take the more trouble-free, acceptable road of love and marriage.

As girls begin to reach puberty, their bodies and their dreams begin to change, and their freedom and independence are at risk. It is not safe for them to be on the streets alone; they can be harassed, attacked, even abducted. They feel more vulnerable as their female organs develop and they begin to menstruate. Some girls experience uncomfortable symptoms of menstruation such as headaches, tiredness, cramps, and the rather messy and frightening problem of bleeding. As their breasts develop, they may become ill at ease with their changing bodies, causing them to feel anxious, afraid, even sick. While girls are feeling less secure, more fragile, and not so powerful, boys at the same age are beginning to feel "their oats," their aggressiveness, their sexuality, their competitive spirit. Sports, which gives them physical power and a sense of themselves, can become very important to boys during this time. It's encouraging to note that more girls are involved in sports and competitive games these days, so they too are gaining confidence in their abilities along with a sense of vitality and energy.

During adolescence, girls tend to lose ground in their intellectual pursuits. Sometimes they aren't encouraged to compete in academics, or they are given both subtle and direct messages that boys won't like them if they are too smart. Some girls are given extra chores at home that boys might not have, such as helping with housework, cooking, and caring for siblings. It's not surprising that many adolescent girls go through periods when they feel bored, defeated, and debilitated. Their sense of freedom and their enthusiasm for life have been beaten down. They begin to feel inferior to boys and to act that way. At this age, girls (as well as boys) can easily turn to activities that they think will anesthetize their confusion and insecurity, such as drugs, alcohol, or promiscuity. Although these activities may seem like a way for them to gain power, they are closely tied to a plummeting self-esteem.

In the end, even the strongest, most confident adolescent girls realize that men's brute force still has it over them, and they are compelled to live with the ever-present awareness and fear of being attacked or raped by an overpowering man.

At the same time, having boys around as friends becomes more important for girls. It doesn't take long before they realize that in order to get boys, they have to figure out ways to please and win them over, and they may have to turn over some of their personal power to them. Although many of the rules are changing in today's reality, some girls still follow an old one: If they want to attract boys, they must not be too strong, too brainy, too daring, or they will be in danger of driving them away. To be really attractive, girls need to be feminine, pretty, and sexy. Being a bit weak and helpless might also help. Moreover, they should at least appear interested in what boys enjoy.

Without a doubt, adolescence is a very difficult time for girls. Not only do their bodies change radically, but they are no longer as free and powerful as they had been. At this point, they have to make a decision: Will they become more passive and "feminine" or will they rebel against what might appear to them as subjugation and oppression? Most girls give in to the magnetic pull of being sought after by the dominant male. It doesn't take long before they are obsessed with how they look, how to wear their hair, how to use makeup, how their bodies are shaped, how to be attractive. They spend hours of their time looking into mirrors and primping themselves for boys.

When girls start to look for "their man," they are hungry to know what love is all about and how they will respond to it. They often dream about finding someone who will take them away from their dreary existence. During this stage, their relationships with their girlfriends may change. Initially most girls turn to their best friends to discuss their romantic fantasies. They hammer out every detail of an imaginary love affair with someone who will hold the key to their happiness. They imagine themselves being secure in the arms of a man, much as they remember feeling when they were children in their fathers' arms.

Because they are overwhelmed by and somewhat afraid of boys, some girls turn their fantasies and affections toward older female teachers, movie stars, or other women whom they admire. Others choose to focus on men who feel "safe" to them: sports heroes, rock stars, professors, ministers, even married men who are friends of the family. Usually these men are not threatening to them nor do they burst their fantasy bubbles. Some women never leave this adolescent stage of inventing "the perfect man." They continue to look for someone who will be all things for them, who will adore them, but not require much back from them. They refuse to see men as they are with their good and bad qualities, with their strengths and shortcomings. How often we hear women say, "I want a man who will always take care of me." "When I have my man, I will never have to worry." "I dream of feeling safe in my man's arms." Could they be looking for their daddy?

Eventually most adolescent girls accept the rules of society, give up their earlier idealistic dreams, and enter their new life. By the age of fourteen or fifteen, most of them have already gone through puberty, menstruation, sexual awakenings, fears of and yearnings for love. And they may have learned how to hide some of their feelings. De Beauvoir writes, "The lie to which the adolescent girl is condemned is that she must pretend to be an object, and a fascinating one. . . . Make-up, false hair, girdles, and 'reinforced' brassieres are all lies. The very face itself becomes a mask."[3]

As girls begin to go out with boys, their relationships with their girlfriends are still important to them. They get advice from each other; learn from each others' experiences, successes, and failures; plot out possible plans to capture boys' interest; and plan revenge on boyfriends who have hurt them. Fifteen-year-old Jana spoke of her early experiences of dating: "When I started going out, it was really fun to talk about my dates with my friend Bonnie. While I was out on a date, I memorized every little detail of what happened, so I could tell Bonnie later. I could hardly wait to get home to call her on the phone. Sometimes I woke her up. But she didn't care. 'Tell me every detail and don't leave out a thing.' At times we giggled so hard about the crazy things that happened that I woke up my parents. I think we had more fun talking about our boyfriends than we actually had being with them."

But other girls discover that they can't talk about their boyfriends with their friends, because they are maturing differently. This can be quite stressful on their friendships. Betsy verbalized some of her struggles with her friend: "When I was sixteen, I started going out with a guy who was in his twenties. My girlfriend Camilla couldn't understand what I was going through or what I was feeling. She kept warning me that I might get hurt or that I was getting too involved with him. When she started giving me advice and asking too many questions, I really resented it. She didn't understand what he meant to me or how I had changed. I felt so much older than her. Eventually we grew apart and we're not really close anymore."

As young women mature and become adults, most of them continue to prepare themselves for their man. They work hard at winning the attention and love of what they hope will be the ideal man. They want to be ready for a relationship with "Mr. Right." Some women even compete with their friends and sacrifice their friendships for a man. Thus when a woman does fall in love with a man, she may believe that her life has been transformed, that she is beautiful, sensual, elegant, valued. She may see the world through the eyes of her "Prince Charming." She prefers the music and food he likes, reads what he reads, becomes interested in his ideas and in the places he wants to visit.

As a woman begins to live in her man's world, her own universe may crumble, her friendships disintegrate, her options disappear. But it doesn't seem to matter to a woman in love. If she thinks she is loved by her man, she feels that she is fulfilled and happy—even if she is miserable. If she thinks her man loves her less than he should or if she fails to satisfy him, she may chastise herself for being inadequate, for not trying hard enough to be what he wants. If a woman feels desperate that she doesn't have a man in her life, she will do anything to hitch herself to one—even if he isn't someone she wants to be with.

If a woman is starved for love, it's easy for any man to arouse her undying ardor and devotion.

Dot, one of my girlfriends who was single and thirty-five, was quite desperate to find a man. Each time she started a new relationship, she threw her energy into making it work, hoping this would be "the one." Several times she told me that a new man was in her life and that she would get back in touch with me when the relationship was on solid ground or after it had ended. That translated as: A relationship with a man is the most important thing; a friendship with a woman ranks as second best. After one of these announcements, I told Dot that I would not be waiting around when she returned. If she didn't value our friendship enough to stay in contact while she worked out things with the new man, we honestly didn't have a real relationship. Fortunately she heard what I said, and we managed to hang onto our friendship. She is now happily married, and we are still good friends.

A negative theme often portrayed in films and books relates to the fear that many women share: that their closest girlfriends—the very people they trust and confide in—will betray them. They are concerned that friends who learn all the details about their boyfriends will know how to steal those sweethearts from them. The words from *The Tennessee Waltz* come to mind: "Introduced her to my darlin' and while they were dancin', my friend stole my sweetheart from me." Certainly we hear numerous stories about how a woman's closest friend runs off with her husband, sometimes with her husband and her children. It can and does happen.

Paige, a beautiful forty-three-year-old landscape designer in Annapolis, talks about her painful experience with her best friend. "When my friend went through a devastating divorce, I felt sorry for her and invited her to stay for a few months in our home while she got her act together. She was grateful that I offered to help her, and she got along well with my husband and our three young children. After my friend had been with us for nearly six months, my husband told me that he no longer loved me, that he had fallen in love with my friend, and he wanted a divorce. I was absolutely shocked and devastated. When I confronted my friend, she refused to talk with me about the situation.

"Not long after my husband and I were divorced, they were married and moved to another state leaving me with our three young children and not a penny of child support. I had not planned ahead, so I didn't have adequate financial resources to pay the mortgage and bills on our new home. I had to move to a tiny apartment with my children, and eventually I was forced to declare bankruptcy. It was a very difficult time for me. I felt betrayed and angry. I doubt that I will ever trust another woman friend again—certainly not around a man that I care about."

It's sad to note that Paige did not say she would *never trust another man* again—*only* a woman friend. Actually this kind of tale of betrayal is not as prevalent as we think. Terri Apter and Ruthellen Josselson write in *Best Friends*, "Yet such commonly portrayed and commonly feared triangles aren't, in fact, common. . . . It is the fear, not the frequency, of such betrayals that makes them a common theme in novels and films. The image of a girlfriend taking what we want from us registers our continuing sense of how dangerous these usually comfortable and comforting attachments can be."[4]

Perhaps we should consider what may be a somewhat camouflaged "threat" to women's relationships: *men themselves*. Men may realize how important and potent women's friendships could be. Possibly they understand that women friends could become a powerful support team and together turn into their own liberators or "knights in shining armor." Therefore, men may encourage women to treat them (men) and their friends as more important than women by subtly minimizing and belittling women's friendships. As Apter and Josselson write, "And so it is that women's friendships are often endangered by the larger social order in which values are set by men who have learned that if they manage to keep women divided, they will maintain their power over them. . . . As long as some men continue to regard women's bonds as threatening, they will refuse to acknowledge their existence except in skeptical, condescending terms."[5] A very interesting concept to consider!

Early in my adult life, I fell madly in love with a man I thought was perfect. I didn't allow him to have any flaws or weaknesses. In my eyes he could do no wrong. With a little encouragement from him, I turned him into a hero, an impossibly wonderful person—right up there with God. I was willing to go anywhere he wanted to go, do anything he wanted to do, become whatever he wanted me to be. I supported this man no matter what he did or said. If he insulted someone or did something hurtful or stupid, I defended him, stood behind and in front of him. Just like the words of the Rodgers and Hammerstein song "Something Wonderful" from *The King and I*, "You'll always go along, defend him when he's wrong, and tell him when he's strong, he is wonderful." Yes, that's exactly what I did.

One of the saddest parts of this story is that I allowed him to push away some of my closest girlfriends, women I thoroughly enjoyed having in my life. If he didn't want them around, he had a way of saying rather subtle but nasty things to them, which made them feel uncomfortable. When they attempted to talk with me about this, I wouldn't hear of it. Over time they started drifting away. And eventually so did he. How disappointing and distressing to be forced to realize that this man had feet of clay, that indeed he was not up there with God, and that we probably never had been very compatible. But I certainly worked hard to keep him on his lofty pedestal and to be what I thought this "ideal man" might want me to be. Fortunately I'm older and wiser now and I've learned to respect and care for myself, to look at and accept men for who and what they are—not for what I want them to be or for what they might hope I would see in them. More important, I've come to value my friendships with women too much to allow a relationship with a man to come between us in such a negative way.

I believe the world would be a better place for everyone if women's friendships were more valued—by men and by women—if they weren't treated in condescending ways and torn apart—by men and by women. Certainly that's an aspiration worth striving for.

Benefiting from Men and Friendships

• •

Where men really "come between us" is through
the time they take away from our friends and the
relative importance they expect—or are granted.
Terri Apter and Ruthellen Josselson[6]

Healthy relationships with men can be superb—almost astonishing. Men can add stability, security, companionship, joy, excitement, and spice to life. But at times they wreak havoc on a woman's world and especially on her friendships. If we do not understand this, we might be at risk of losing our valuable and supportive relationships with women. Here's what some levelheaded women have suggested as possible ideas to help us enrich our relationships with men and women and to resolve problems that may arise related to men and friendships.

*Are you a whole person with or
without a relationship with a man?*

Many women believe they are not a whole person if they don't have a man in their lives. Certainly a *healthy* relationship with a man can be a truly exceptional experience that adds something wonderful to our lives. Even so, it is only one part of our life, along with other special parts such as family members, meaningful work, avocations, and friendships. Having a relationship with a man may or may not add to who and what we are. If we are able to identify and pursue our own goals and priorities in life, we become more whole—both inside and outside our relationships.

Do you expect too much of a relationship with a man?

Even a strong relationship with a man cannot be all things for us. If we have too many expectations of our connection with a man or we are too dependent on him, we could be in for some rough times. Most men don't want to be the sole provider of support in a relationship; it's overwhelming. Also we may discover that a man alone is not capable of meeting all of our needs, that there are pieces of our life that are lacking. Although we may tell ourselves that we are not lonely and that a man is all we need, we may find ourselves emotionally hungry. When we have realistic expectations of our relationships with men and maintain some healthy friendships with women too, we will avoid being disappointed that a man couldn't be everything we wanted him to be.

Do you dump your girlfriends
when you are involved with a man?

Many women value relationships with men more than they do with women. So when a man walks into a woman's life, she may dump her girlfriends. Research reports point out that married women who maintain their female friendships are physically and emotionally healthier than those who don't. These relationships take some of the pressure off marriages that may be filled with a lot of stress—which in today's world is quite common. Other studies show that women live longer because of their friendships. So even when we are head over heels in love, it's better not to dump our girlfriends; they may be tremendously helpful and supportive to us. As one woman says, "When a man leaves—and he usually does at some stage in your life, be grateful if you have a good female friend in your life. She will help you through thick and thin." So let's hang on to our healthy relationships with women since they just might be life savers and life givers.

Can you choose a man who is open
to your having close female friends?

If we are involved with a man who is threatened by our having female friends, we may want to pay attention to this and try to understand what is going on. A man doesn't have to like our friends the way we do or want to spend time with them. But it helps if he understands that they play a significant role in our life. If he's not open to this, we may want to consider looking for another man who welcomes our having women friends who also support and care for us.

*Do you understand that men
are different, not necessarily better?*

If men are viewed as superior to women, it is logical that
women will not be perceived as valuable as men. Therefore,
women will not be treated as equals nor will they feel like
equals. If we believe our man is exceptional and extraordinary,
he probably will think he has the right to be treated as special
and expect us to do that. Once we get up close and personal
with a man, we will learn that he is not better than we are—
just different. After all, he too is an imperfect, mortal human
being—just like we are.

*Do you think you are valuable
and, therefore, deserve a good man?*

Having a healthy and satisfying relationship with a man
starts with how we feel about ourselves. We may have been told
by someone that we are "only a girl," and therefore we assume
we're not as good as a man. If we recognize that females (like
males) are competent, gifted, and loaded with endless potential, then we will understand that we are not second-rate,
mediocre, or inferior; rather, we are high-quality, worthy people. When we accept this as truth, we won't allow ourselves to
be involved in unhealthy or harmful relationships. So let's not
settle for a negative or detrimental relationship with any man
who happens to show up on our screen. We are eligible to have
one that is first rate—just like we are.

Are you able to develop your own resources?

It's a blessing to share our lives with a generous man who
takes good care of us. But we need to have our own resources
so we can be self-sufficient and independent, should we need
to be. We can't count on a man (or anyone for that matter)
being with us forever. He may leave, get sick, or even die before
we do. If we have our own assets, including supportive friends,
we will be in a more advantageous position, no matter what
happens. By identifying and developing our resources, we
won't fall into the trap of thinking a man will take care of all
our needs for our entire lives.

Can you get out of a bad relationship?

Many women stay in terrible, sometimes abusive, relationships because they are afraid they will be alone, they won't meet another man, or they "have nowhere to go." Other women blame themselves for whatever goes wrong within their relationships. They are concerned that if they speak up or confront their man, he will get annoyed and leave. If this happens to us, we need to make some changes. We may want to consider asking for professional help. Also, this is a good time to call on our supportive women friends to rally around us through what could be some very tough times. We should always remember that we deserve to have healthy, fulfilling relationships with men and with women.

*Can you help ensure that girls
and women will be valued in the future?*

The world is in so much trouble that we can no longer waste the precious human resources of girls and women. Institutions, religious organizations, societies, and governments should do everything possible to ensure that girls and women will be respected as valuable people who have much to contribute in the universe. We need every person working together as equals to make this a better place for everyone.

Today we realize that friendship provides additional sources of intimacy and a reinforcement of self-worth necessary throughout the adult married years.

Jan Yager[7]

RECOGNIZING

needs and feelings

TEN .

The mere idea of mentioning a hurt, expressing a grievance, showing a friend that she has made one angry . . . can make a woman very nervous.

Luise Eichenbaum and Susie Orbach[1]

When a female begins her life as a baby, she experiences a whole range of feelings. She is free to express whatever comes to her mind, whatever she feels. So she speaks her mind, and she speaks the truth. When she is happy, she blissfully wiggles and giggles. If she is sad, she cries. When she is angry, she flails out kicking and screaming. Her body and her feelings are in harmony with each other and are appropriately interconnected.

But somewhere along the way, this picture changes for girls. Parents, teachers, society, and religious institutions impart messages to young girls about what are "appropriate" ways to express their feelings and their needs, about what is tolerable for them to do and what is not. It doesn't take long before girls become sensitive to peoples' reactions, and they realize that it's not "nice" to communicate feelings that are "bad" or disagreeable. And so they do what they've learned is the "right thing"—what will please someone. Furthermore, girls can easily see that when a boy is hurt it's not suitable for him to cry, because he might be called a sissy or "a girl"—and being thought of as "a girl" is obviously something negative. However, it's not a problem if he screams and yells when he is angry. In contrast, when a girl is hurt or angry, yelling and screaming are considered unattractive or inappropriate and, therefore, unacceptable. So girls learn it is best to be nice and to cry when they are afraid, angry, upset, or hurt.

Without a doubt, our society encourages girls (and later women) not to make waves, to "go along with things" in order to "get along." Girls who speak out boldly or truthfully can be viewed as pushy, loud-mouthed, and not nice. In an environment where agreeing with the rules of being female is still rewarded, girls become skilled at being sweet and pleasing people in order to be tolerated and liked. When I taught students in the elementary grades, I noticed that at recess time most of the girls played non-confrontational games, courteously took turns, and cooperated with each other. Or they talked and laughed in groups around the edge of the playground. Meanwhile, the boys played rougher contact games, called each other names, argued and yelled loudly, and easily made up after their fights. In the classroom, girls were mild-mannered, polite, and not as aggressive as boys. In discussions with other educators, they too reported that young girls (this can be quite different in older girls) tend to listen, express agreement, compliment one another, and let others enter into their conversations. On the other hand, boys are more inclined to show off, brag, interrupt each other, give orders, and refuse to do as they're told.

It's not difficult to understand why girls and women begin to have doubts about the value of their own thoughts or ideas. As Patricia Lynn Reilly writes: "We were required to be nice and pleasant at the expense of our own healthy integrity . . . we learned to question our truth and to defer to the thoughts and perceptions of others, assuming something was wrong with us."[2]

As girls grow older, they may act inferior or subordinate to men and tend to speak submissively and with less authority. Often their language is not clear, straightforward, or precise, so their communications can be confusing and cause misunderstandings in their relationships. Judith Selee McClure describes some of the common traits of women's "feminine," non-assertive speech.

- Is indirect and imprecise
- Uses more nonverbal communication (gesture and intonation)
- Rarely commits to an opinion
- Asks questions rather than makes assertions
- Tends to make emotional rather than logical statements
- Frequently asks for permission or approval.[3]

The desire to be seen as "good enough" also brings on other problems for females. They can be overly sensitive to anything that seems to be "wrong" about them, so words directed at them that appear to be judgmental or negative become personal attacks. Because they desperately want to please and win approval, they may become defensive when they are given suggestions or are criticized. This can cause difficulties when women work in highly competitive workplaces; they may be unable to handle situations that are demanding or that require high performance standards. Some women come unglued and easily fall apart when they are evaluated or critiqued, believing that they are never able to be good enough.

As we saw earlier in "Our Mother, Our First Friend," many women are encumbered with unfinished business from disappointments and hurts they experienced with their mothers. Therefore, they look for acceptance, support, and love in their friendships with other women. With so much riding on these interactions succeeding, women tend to be cautious about discussing any aspects of their relationships that are negative or disagreeable for them. If they express their feelings or speak the truth, they are afraid their friends will reject or discard them, not unlike their mothers. They also worry that they will be seen as selfish or unkind if they say what is on their minds. Because of these and other concerns, many women find it difficult to talk openly about problems with one another. So they try to speculate what the other person is thinking rather than checking in with her or verbalizing their concerns. Even worse, they begin to imagine that they are being criticized, rejected, or that they are the brunt of their friend's anger, even though none of this may be accurate. Thus the relationship can be seriously damaged with little or no trust remaining between the friends.

Without a doubt, women's interactions suffer because of unclear and ambiguous communications. Many more are harmed, even destroyed, because disagreements, misunderstandings, and hurts remain unspoken, rather than being clarified and appropriately vented. Sometimes women remove themselves from a relationship without first undergoing a reality test to determine if a problem actually exists. Many friendships are broken without either of the friends ever talking about what happened.

To avoid the possibility of a friendship slipping away and disappearing, talking over problems is very important, perhaps critical. Luise Eichenbaum and Susie Orbach add that speaking up is not just about being honest about our feelings; "it has the more crucial function, potentially, to challenge the projections we may well be making. Projections are a transaction in which, without realizing it, one sees (projects) a part of oneself in the other. We describe another's behavior or translate another's behavior either based on what we wish to be doing but can't see ourselves doing (we imagine they are angry when we are unable to express our own anger), or we load on to them responses from our past that may not be appropriate (we are angry and we imagine they will cut us off if we express it)."[4]

Francesca, who is in her forties and lives in San Diego, talks about a conflict she experienced with her friend Lolita. "We were best friends for more than ten years and worked as secretaries in the same office building. Every day we went to lunch together. We were very close. Then one day I noticed that Lolita was acting strange toward me, definitely different from the way she usually was. She seemed distanced, like she wasn't glad to see me or interested in talking. She started saying she didn't have time to go to lunch because she had errands to do. I tried not to get upset, but it shook me up. This went on for several weeks. One day I asked her, 'What's wrong, Lolita? We haven't talked for a long time. I don't understand what's happening.' She just shrugged her shoulders and raised her eyebrows like she didn't have a clue what I was talking about. Then she shook her head and stared at me like I was crazy. That really threw me for a loop.

"After about six weeks, I couldn't stand it any longer. I waited for Lolita outside our office building and walked with her to the bus. 'Okay, Lolita, you've been my best friend for a long time. You have to tell me what's going on. Are you all right? Have I done something wrong?' I was surprised when she said, 'I can't deal with your anger and rejection any longer. It feels like I can never do anything right for you. I don't want to be around you anymore.' I was shocked, because none of what Lolita said about me had one ounce of truth in it. But no matter what I said to her, she just kept saying that I was angry and critical of her. She told me to stay away from her, that she didn't want to be around my pessimism and my negative energy, that she didn't want to be friends with me anymore. Eventually I gave up and we're no longer friends.

"Much later I found out that Lolita was going through some tough times herself. Maybe she was angry at me for not figuring that out. But how could I know that if she didn't tell me? It makes me sad and upset that she wasn't willing to talk honestly and tell me what was really happening. I think we could have worked things out and saved our friendship. Now I feel like I have a big hole in my heart and in my life."

Certainly this kind of break can be very painful, especially if one friend makes a decision to end the friendship without giving the other an opportunity to talk over what happened, what might have been misunderstood, or what could have been changed. Sometimes this kind of treatment can be brutal and heartless, almost vindictive. As Francine Prose writes, "A loss of this sort leaves a void that is impossible to fill, since it is impossible to recreate the quirks and qualities, the gifts and strengths, and even flaws, that draw us to a particular person, that move us to choose one person, rather than another, as our friend." [5]

Francesca and Lolita's story is a vivid example of how projection and poor communication can harm friendships. Francesca may have been the target of Lolita's anger and hostility, but without talking it through, both women ended up losing and suffering. According to Suzy Hansen, "Friends pride themselves on being able to understand everything about their counterparts. . . . Being shut out is almost like being killed off—for both parties."[6]

Another problem that often emerges in women's relationships is caused by their intense need to be helpful and their craving to belong. Women see themselves as being empathetic and supportive—especially with close friends. Their desire to be in an amicable relationship with other women makes it difficult for them to express any feelings that don't seem to be supportive or in agreement with those of their friends. Although girls and women argue with their boyfriends and their husbands, they rarely quarrel, disagree, or express disapproving thoughts with their female friends, even when they have been selfish, mean, or thoughtless. Usually they end up agreeing with them, although they may have a completely opposite point of view.

Eichenbaum and Orbach write about the problems that can arise around the issue of empathetic "commiseration," which they describe as "an integral part of women's highly developed repertoire of giving . . . the capacity to show that one understands what another might be feeling and comforting her."[7] If a woman only commiserates with her friend about a problem, even if she sees it in another way or has an idea for a solution, it will likely remain as it has been, since commiseration does not challenge or criticize. The words "I know how you feel" are too easily said and often are not very helpful. For some women, they can only commiserate with their friends because they do not have strong enough boundaries to take a stand on their own (see "The Plus of Boundaries").

Consequently many women take on their friends' problems as though they are their own.

When a woman does get up the courage to speak to her friend in a critical or disapproving way, she takes a risk. There is always a possibility that her friend will be upset, perhaps furious, with her for "attacking" her and not being supportive. And if the relationship breaks up, the woman who took the risk could end up feeling guilty. For women who have been genuine friends for some time, this usually does not occur. Women who are able to talk honestly and openly with each other regarding problems or negative feelings have a good chance at not only salvaging their friendship but perhaps deepening it. A suggestion, an honest opinion, even a direct confrontation with a friend offers the possibility that some kind of resolution for a difficult situation can be found.

Claire, a medical technician in her mid-twenties in Kansas City, spoke about her friendship with Teri. "We met in college and became close buddies from the first time we talked. We had so much in common. We laughed and cried our way through boyfriends, exams, graduate work. It felt like we were always there supporting each other in everything we did. Quite early on we made a pledge to speak honestly with one another, even if it was difficult.

"At one point in our friendship, I felt like Teri had not been there for me, that she had really let me down. I admit I didn't want to confront her, to tell her that she had hurt me, and that I was disappointed and upset. I wasn't accustomed to telling women anything negative. Even the thought of it made me uncomfortable. I felt myself starting to drift away from our friendship. I imagined how I would 'punish' her and leave her stewing in her own mess. But then I came to my senses. I knew I didn't want to do that, because she had been a true friend for such a long time. How could I ever replace her friendship?

"For quite a while, I avoided saying anything to Teri because I was concerned that I didn't know the best way to tell her what I was feeling or that I would say the wrong thing. And if she misunderstood, I could hurt her and make matters worse. Finally I realized how important it was for us to talk about this, to try to work it through together. I hoped it would make our friendship stronger. So I got up my courage to talk with her. I tried not to make her feel defensive, not to *accuse* her of letting me down, but to tell her that I *felt* let down. Teri was much more open to what I had to say than I thought she would be. In fact, I think she was relieved that I brought up the problem and opened the door to having it resolved. This encounter has really strengthened our relationship. Now we are much more willing to express our concerns and to air problems that come up between us rather than letting them simmer under the pretense that all is well. I'm confident that in the future we will continue to talk with each other about our feelings and our needs. Certainly our inability and our unwillingness to say what we felt almost caused our friendship to fail. I doubt that we will ever be in danger of losing our friendship again."

Recognizing Needs and Feelings

Women have found that using traditional feminine speech seems to leave them behind. . . . But they have also found that borrowing traditionally masculine speech often produces a backlash.
Judith Selee McClure[8]

By not verbalizing our needs and feelings, we run into many unnecessary obstacles. That is especially true in relationships with our women friends. Nearly all the issues that have been discussed in earlier chapters would likely benefit if we could learn how to appropriately say what we need and feel.

Here are ideas that some highly communicative, straightforward women have tried out in their interactions with friends. They've proved to be helpful in recognizing and verbalizing these women's needs.

Do you know and stand up for your values?

Sometimes women appear to be confused—almost mystified—about who they really are and what they stand for. Out of their desire to be accepted, they try to become what they think others want them to be. If we are able to inform others who we really are and what our genuine values are, we won't be bounced around like tiny boats on a turbulent ocean of other peoples' demands—not a stable place to be. It's important for us to know ourselves and our values and to stand up for them. Most likely people will respect the authentic us more than the counterfeit one. As the singer Janis Joplin once said, "Don't compromise yourself. You're all you've got."

Can you tell others what is not acceptable to you?

Women can get into deep trouble in relationships if they don't know their limits—their "hot spots"—or if they don't tell people about them. When we know what is not tolerable to us, we can tell people and avoid their over-using or abusing us. Then when someone tries to change us, convince us, or fix us, we can meet them head-on and tell them "no." A firmly stated "no" is much better than a wishy-washy "yes." Of course, our friends also have limits, so we need to be aware of and respect those, too.

Can you use direct, unambiguous language at appropriate times?

Sometimes women's speech is so vague that one wonders if it is a reflection of their frame of mind. Or they say things that don't seem to agree with their body language. In order to have healthier relationships, we need to use precise, clear words that communicate what we really mean. Most people will appreciate our not forcing them to guess what we're saying. But whenever we are direct, we need to apply the spiritual practices of compassion and kindness and watch for signs that indicate when it is appropriate to speak and when it is better to wait.

*Are you able to listen actively
and not take things personally?*

Criticism often has a negative impact on women, who find it difficult to let any kind of "disapproval" roll off their backs without getting upset. But if we want to have strong relationships, we have to be willing to listen to each other without jumping to conclusions or getting overly defensive. It's easy to pretend we are listening when we are really preparing our comeback or an argument to defend ourselves. However, that's a sure way to miss what someone is saying to us. Research shows that if we *actively* listen, we will relax, and our blood pressure will go down. That alone might be worth some intense listening. And if we want to stop over-personalizing things, we can start by listening actively and understanding what someone is really saying to us by trying not to become defensive about what is said, and by ceasing to think about what we are going to say in our defense. If we can put some of these ideas into practice, perhaps our blood pressure will go down.

*Do you understand that overly-negative
disapproval may be someone's "stuff"?*

Most people can be offensive, disrespectful, and excessively demanding at some time or another. Sometimes when someone says something nasty to us, it may have very little to do with us. Rather, it may be about that person. That's tough to remember when someone is saying bad things about us or pushing all our buttons. But if we can stay unruffled and ride through the storm, we may be able to work things out later when things are calmer. After we've listened to someone, we may want to weigh in with our thoughtful words, too.

Are you able to air your concerns?

When problems come up, friends need to understand what is happening by talking things over with one another. Airing concerns may seem risky at first, and certainly there are times when that strategy can backfire. But it's a lot better than continuing down the road of confusion and hurt feelings where one or both people end up suffering from frustration, anger, regret, or guilt. And if projection gets added to the mix, the friendship might be in serious danger. When we talk through problems or misunderstandings in a non-guilt-inflicting manner, there's a possibility that we can understand what is happening and begin the process of righting any wrongs.

Can you deal with a friend's anger without running away?

If a relationship is valuable to us, it's worth trying to deal with problems that come up. We might first try to understand what our friend is feeling and why. It's helpful if we don't allow ourselves to assume that we did something wrong, that we are guilty, or that it is our fault. And we don't need to apologize when our friend is upset, because it may not have anything to do with us. By working together to clarify the issues and get more information, we might be able to fix something, if it's fixable.

Can a criticism be growth-producing?

Because women can be thin-skinned and touchy, they are easily hurt and may miss an opportunity for growth. The possibility of learning something about ourselves can be blocked by overreacting to someone's criticism about us. BJ Gallagher writes: "A complaint is really a gift . . . we should thank someone who brings us a complaint. They have given us something valuable, something useful."9 We may want to try looking at criticism or disapproval in a fresh light, as a possible way of learning something new about ourselves.

Do you keep compassion in
confrontations and use "I" language?

It's easy to point a finger at a friend, tear into her, and accuse her of what she has done wrong: "You did this." Although she may not have done anything, to us it may feel like she did. Any time a critical finger is pointed at someone, it's almost certain that person will start slinging accusations right back. Friends may be more open to hearing what we have to say if we tell them how we *feel* about the situation and use "I" language. For example: "I feel hurt when . . ." "I don't feel valued if . . ." and "This situation makes me feel angry." When we express things from this point of view, we are not laying a guilt trip on our friends; rather, the focus is on how actions have an impact on *us*. Our friend might be able to hear us without constructing her own wall of defense. Sometimes we get confused about what it means to be open and honest. Expressing feelings and confronting people are not about attacking them, nor are they about being harsh. Even if we are hurt or angry, it's important to approach our friends with kindness and to give them an opportunity to say what they need to say. It will make a huge difference in the outcome.

Can you listen with a genuine commitment to understand?

Perhaps one of the most important things we can do is to become good listeners. It all starts with our intention to listen well and to truly hear what someone is saying, not what we think they might be saying. If we really hear someone, we will likely be able to correct problems that occur in a friendship. We need to focus only on the things that are in our control to change.

Are you a silent, sacrificial martyr?

Some women think they should not make their wishes known, that it is better to remain quiet about what they need. Perhaps they hope someone will be able to figure out what they want without having to tell them. But most people are not very good at reading another person's mind, or they are too busy dealing with their own stuff to pay attention to people who are silently suffering. If we sacrifice our own requirements for everyone else, we may be headed for a big disillusionment. Most people aren't grateful or appreciative of people who are in the role of martyr. So let's try asking for what we deserve. Being straightforward is a good way to have a better relationship with just about everyone.

A woman who loves herself makes direct statements in response to the requests of others. . . .
With courage and respect for her own life, she no
longer hides her truth within convoluted narratives and indirect explanations.

Patricia Lynn Reilly[10]

SURVIVING THROUGH

friendship

ELEVEN

Give me the support of a few good women
friends, and I can do almost anything.
                    BJ Gallagher[1]

A fter focusing on some of the problems that can
turn up in women's relationships, this chapter
looks at examples of the sheer joy and positive
aspects of women's interactions with each other. In reality,
there are countless stories revealing that women's friendships
can be extraordinary and filled with special gifts, astonishing
deeds, even miracles.

Over the last twenty-five years, I've had the opportunity to
travel, work, and live in many places in the United States and
in countries around the world. Throughout those years, I've
heard many remarkable stories confirming that women do
have a better quality of life because of friendships with
women. There are accounts of women who were given a
friend's kidney to save their lives, of women from all races and
religions who courageously stood beside their friends and
fought for them as they faced dangerous racist or sexist threats
to their existence, of women sharing what little food or money
they had with their impoverished and destitute friends. In
some cases, women might not be alive today if it weren't for
these friendships; they literally helped them to survive. These

stories are more widespread than we can imagine, and they are brimming with compassion and tenderness. This chapter includes five of these inspiring stories that touched my heart and renewed my faith in the tremendous power of women's friendships. I hope they will do the same for you. There are three moving stories from the United States about women whose friendships truly made a difference. In between those narratives are two breathtaking stories from India and Germany.

• •

Whether we are black or white, fat or thin, outgoing or shy, rich or poor, old or young, we are first and foremost female. Our common bond of feminine experience is stronger than any differences.

BJ Gallagher[2]

Joanna

• •

Without the friendship of a group of like-minded women, we couldn't have fought those battles.

Joanna

Joanna is a woman in her late forties who lives with her family in Colorado. Like many other women, she balances motherhood, marriage, volunteerism, and her career. In the mix, however, she always manages to find time for her friendships which she says "are critical in keeping my wheels on the road."

In the late 1970s, on the cusp of Title IX, Joanna was a young athlete at a Division III college. "Our facilities and equipment were dismal compared to the men's. But the intangibles—such as respect and attention for young women who needed and wanted to compete in athletics—were nonexistent. The men's teams and coaches looked at us with scorn or, worse, amusement. After completing a season, we felt almost humiliated by the stuffed animals and trinkets we received. We weren't given the 'real' letters the men got to wear on their jackets.

"A couple of my girlfriends and I complained to one of the deans about our volleyball practices in the decrepit, cramped women's gym: 'The walls are so close and the ceiling is so low, that it's not like playing a real game.' He just rolled his eyes and said, 'If you girls just wouldn't hit the ball so hard, you wouldn't have a problem.' I knew from earlier experiences in high school athletics that young women can gain a sense of confidence when they compete and are recognized for that. I had played fast pitch softball in high school and wanted to play in college, but there was no college team. I started talking with some of my women friends about playing together. We were able to gather a bunch of women—many of whom had never played seriously—and put a rag-tag group together. A few of them joined me in putting pressure on the administration and sports department. We insisted that we needed a coach and a schedule of games.

"Perhaps because of our pressure or perhaps because the administration saw the Title IX writing on the wall, we got what we asked for. I had no idea then that we were one of the stepping stones on the path to what is now a successful women's sports program at the college. At the time, it truly felt like a bunch of close friends just wanting to play a game we loved. I admit we had fun fighting what was clearly an unfair 'good-old-boys' system.

"Without the friendship of a group of like-minded women, we couldn't have fought those battles. It brings tears to my eyes now to see young, strong women and their teams getting star treatment on my alma mater's bulletins and websites. Young women today often take for granted the opportunities they have. They may not realize how many women—both amateur and professional—came before them and fought the battles for their rights and privileges.

"In hindsight, I realize it is often small groups—usually of women friends—who share dreams and goals together, who make small ripples that can turn into cultural waves and change things for the better."

Usha

• •

Nothing is impossible for women—even in India—if they have good friends.
Usha

Usha lives in a tiny house in a village near Baramati in Maharashtra State. Her house is built from durable materials, not the usual mud walls that wash away during the monsoon season. There are plants growing in front of her house, and everything looks quite spotless. As Usha walks out of her house, she exudes a sense of confidence and pride, but it wasn't always that way. Because her family was extremely poor and she was of little value to them as a female, Usha was married when she was eleven to a man who was forty-seven. Her husband was a hardworking man, who owned five acres of land and a bullock. When she was fourteen, Usha was ecstatic when she gave birth to a son, because she knew her husband would be pleased. Almost one year later, her husband was dead from an unknown illness. Usha found herself in a tough predicament: She was a young widow in a village in India, where widows were considered an economic drain and worthless. Both her husband's and her own family deserted her. As a widow, she faced the possibility of poverty, homelessness, starvation, and of men trying to make "good use" of her, as an inconsequential woman. At the time, Usha had no legal right to her husband's land. For several months she worked at weeding other people's fields, her small son always near her. But she barely made enough money to feed her child and herself.

Several women, who often spoke with Usha when they collected water at the village well, became friends with her. They knew bad things could easily happen to her. Although they were well aware that it might be dangerous for them, they decided to take Usha and her son under their wings. Usha's friends became a network of women in the community who helped her. They took turns allowing her to sleep near their tiny mud huts, gave her any extra food they had, and helped her save a few rupees. After a few years of support from her friends, she was able to buy a very small plot of land. It wasn't easy for a seventeen-year-old girl to plow the land, haul bags of seeds, and bring water from the water hole to her dry land. But again, with the help of her friends, she did it. To the surprise of her neighbors, Usha became a good farmer. People began asking her for advice about how to cultivate the land and what seeds to grow. By the time she was twenty-five, rather than being an outcast, she was considered a respected member and leader in her village.

Because Usha's village had no water tap, the women had to walk nearly two miles each morning and evening to get water for cooking, drinking, and bathing. Usha heard that the government would install water taps in villages, but it usually took influential people or money to get them to act. Obviously the women had neither. As they talked about the problem, Usha suggested that the women take their children and enough food for several days to the water commissioner's office where they would hold a "sit-in." At first the authorities ignored the women and children sitting on the veranda outside the office. But at the end of the day when the office was closing, they were still there and refused to leave until they could see the commissioner. He agreed to see them in two days. The women said that was fine, but they would stay on the veranda until their appointment. The next day, the commissioner met with them and promised them the water tap. After four months and three more "sit-ins," the tap was finally installed in their village.

Today Usha still farms her land. She is regarded as a leader by both men and women in her community. Her friends are very proud of her and continue to be supportive of her, as she is of them. She is impressive as she walks with self-assurance around her land and in the village. Through the assistance of her friends, she has become strong and courageous. "Women need to understand that it is important to be friends and help one another, as we do here," declares Usha. "Nothing is impossible for women—even in India—if they have good friends."

Bella

• •

I thank God every day for my friend who saved our life and helped us start a new one.
Bella

Bella and her family were residents in New Orleans for generations. Her great grandparents had lived in the same house that Bella and her four children were living in when her husband left her in 1998. "It was really hard for me to make ends meet after my husband moved out. I had to earn enough to pay the bills and feed my four kids. Two of them were already teenagers and big eaters. I worked as a cleaning lady in rich peoples' houses who lived in the suburbs of the city. I had to leave early in the morning on the bus, and often I got home really late. I was always worried about my kids, about what would happen to them, what trouble they might get into. I was especially concerned that they would start doing bad street things.

"You can't imagine how thankful I felt when my friend Nell, a widow who lives down the street from me, offered to come to my house early in the morning to help get the kids off to school. Then she made them come to her house after school to do their homework, and she almost always ended up feeding them something. When I stopped by after work, she insisted that I have 'a little bite to eat' too. I don't think she had that much more money than me, but she was one of those really generous friends who cared about me like a younger sister. And she was willing to help me in any way possible. She always said, 'Don't worry about paying me back, I know you'll be there when I need you.' Of course, that was true.

"Nell was a retired nurse who had worked in one of the city's hospitals for years, so she was always on my case about my ten-year-old daughter Lucy's problems with asthma. She kept pushing me to get her to the doctor and to get her medicine. Sometimes she questioned if I had refilled the prescription. Several times she went to the pharmacy to pick it up for me. She even insisted on having an extra bottle around: 'You never know when you might need it.' That ended up being exactly right.

"When Hurricane Katrina was headed for New Orleans, I heard about it on TV. Because Florida did okay when it hit there, we thought it wouldn't be too bad. On TV, they warned people to be careful, that we should go to a place that was on higher ground, if possible. But most of my neighbors were staying. And where would I go with all my kids? And how would we get there? There weren't any special buses or trucks picking up people.

"I talked with Nell, who told me to move my family in with her during the storm because her house was a little bigger and stronger than mine. She told me to bring blankets, food, and water. She insisted that I have my daughter's extra medicine too—just in case.

"Everybody knows how bad Katrina ended up being. And they saw on their TV's what happened to New Orleans. My little house was completely under water, and it was totally destroyed. It was a good thing that we went to Nell's house, because it's a little higher than my house and it has an attic. We went up there as soon as the water started to rise. Nell always was calm and full of ideas about how we could survive. Because she had been a nurse, she knew that we needed to have plenty of water, so she had plastic bottles of water for us to drink. She rationed them out so they lasted a long time. She also had a lot of food in her house, including some really healthy stuff. She said we had to stay strong.

"On the fourth day, we were able to break a hole through the roof of the attic and get out on it. I was really scared that my kids or I would fall into the water and drown. None of us know how to swim. Nell made us take our sheets and blankets and tie them into ropes. She wanted to be sure that every one of us was tied to something when we got out on the roof. Thank God, we were rescued that day.

"It's really amazing what a great friend Nell is. While we were waiting, she got us all to sing hymns and pray together. She kept saying that we were special people, that she loved us, and that we were in God's hands. And she told us that when this was over, she would try to help us get back on our feet again, that it wouldn't be too bad. Nell made me feel hopeful, even when things were really terrible.

"Now we are trying to start our lives again. Nell invited my family to move with her for a while to her sister's home, which is north of New Orleans. She said it was important that we didn't move to another state that would be far away from our family and friends. So that's what we did. Sometimes I can't believe how blessed I am to have such a wonderful friend, a woman who treats me like a sister and really cares for me and my family. Without her, I believe my family and I would have been separated and sent off to different states as refugees. I'm afraid it would have destroyed us. I thank God every day for my friend who saved our life and helped us start a new one."

Johanna

• •

It was the strength and love of my girlfriends that kept me alive.

Johanna

In 1938, when the Nazis first marched into Austria, Johanna's parents were Jewish shopkeepers. Her parents were caught up in the challenges of their business and initially were not conscious of the danger they would soon face. As non-Aryans, they were registered, were under constant observation, and had to wear the yellow Jewish star on their clothes. As time went by, they heard that they could be sent to a concentration camp if they violated the rules. One day when Johanna was visiting her friends Anna and Sophia, they were loaded into a van by soldiers and taken to an open field, where hundreds of Jews were being separated into groups by age and sex. Johanna felt panicked because her parents and siblings were not there. Several days later, she and her friends were marched out of town.

"We were hungry, thirsty, and full of fear as we walked toward an unknown destination. With little rest, food, and water, we soon lost our energy. But we saw that anyone who couldn't walk was shot and left on the side of the road. Although I felt my heart was breaking because I feared the worst for my family, my girlfriends encouraged me not to give up. They said my family would likely be at the place where we were going, and we would be reunited. At times I felt so exhausted that I wanted to stop walking, but Anna and Sophia put me in between them and almost dragged me along. One morning we were shoved into some cattle cars of a freight train. Then we knew we were on our way to a concentration camp. I don't know how long we traveled before the train finally stopped. When the doors were opened, we were near a concentration camp in Germany.

"Anna and Sophia stayed very near me at the camp and kept telling me that somehow we would get through this. When we were given shabby clothes to wear, they said I was stunning in my new outfit. They teased me saying that I would probably meet a good-looking young man in prison who would fall in love with me. At night we slept in racks of wooden boxes stacked on top of each other in our block. The three of us slept together in one box. I remember how Anna laughed saying we were like sardines in a can. Although we had no pillows or blankets, we stayed close together to keep warm. Each morning we had to stand outside our block for inspection. If anyone couldn't stand during that time, they were in danger of being sent away—probably to their death. Many days I was sure I would fall apart, but my friends helped hold me up as they begged and coaxed me into hanging on a little longer.

"Although we had no idea what date it was, when Sophia said it was near our birthdays, she and Anna started making plans for 'celebrations.' Whenever we had a chance, we talked about what kind of cake we wanted, the wine we would drink. It gave us something to look forward to, to dream about. We almost felt normal. On the day of the celebration, we imagined we had a cake with candles and the best wine. It was transforming.

"One morning I woke up with a high fever and severe diarrhea and had to go to the infirmary. Late on the third night, Anna and Sophia crawled through the window of the infirmary and came to my bed. I was shocked to see them. 'We have to get you out of here,' Anna whispered. 'We've heard they're going to empty the infirmary tonight to make room for more people.' I was so sick and hopeless, I didn't really care. I just wanted to give up. But my friends wouldn't let me. They pulled me out of bed, through the window, and dragged me back to our block. Fortunately no one saw us. That night the infirmary was emptied. Without a doubt, I'm alive today because my friends saved my life that night.

"I don't remember much about the last months in the camp, just that we were terribly hungry, weak, and sick. Every day more people died. Several months before I was rescued and set free, both Anna and Sophia became extremely ill with vomiting, dysentery, and high fevers. They died only a few weeks apart. I was devastated. What kept me hanging on was that I could hear things they had said to me, 'We are friends forever. We will stay alive to meet our families again. We must never give up hope. We will survive.' I know it was the strength and love of my girlfriends that kept me alive. After their deaths, I couldn't give up; I had to live—for my friends."

Ginny

• •

The legacy of our friendship will carry on through more than our lives.

Joy

Ginny and I first became friends in junior high school after my family moved from our farm to Lincoln, Nebraska. Ginny was one of the kind and considerate girls who accepted and befriended me when I was simply a country bumpkin straight off the farm without a clue how to survive. When I was terrified that I would drown in the vast challenges of the alien world of algebra, French, competition, multiple choices, hundreds of classmates, and boys, Ginny offered her friendship by showing me the ropes and helping me learn how to become a somewhat acceptable ninth-grade girl in a city school.

After high school, both of us attended Nebraska Wesleyan University, where we remained close friends, pledging the same sorority and rooming together. After graduation, Ginny married and moved to California, and I headed out to Pakistan to work for the United Methodist Church in the slums of Karachi, a place that was filled with challenges, but which I grew to love. Over the years, I lived and worked in many places and survived various difficulties, including some close calls with life-threatening experiences. Whenever I contacted Ginny, she was accessible and supportive to me with her constant generous spirit. I knew I could count on her no matter what.

Although Ginny and I never lived in the same location after we graduated from college, she seemed to show up every time I needed her—during both happy and sad times. When I graduated from seminary, she was there with her camera documenting the joyous occasion. Often when I was the guest speaker or teacher at an important event, I looked into the audience and saw Ginny sitting in a spot where I could easily see her encouraging face. Following my brain tumor surgery in 1993, after my dad and sister Shirley returned to California, Ginny arrived at my apartment in Richmond ready to help out should I need her. Years later when my beloved ninety-six-year-old dad died early in 2005, Ginny was there, standing beside me, her arm around me as Daddy's coffin was lowered into the ground.

It doesn't seem to matter where we are or what we do, our friendship has not only survived, but it has flourished and become more meaningful for both of us. Now I have the special honor of being the godmother of one of Ginny's daughters, Susan Joy. So the legacy of our friendship will carry on through more than our lives.

● ●

Friendship. It's something many people take for granted. They are unaware how powerful and positive friendship can be. . . . The right friends can help you feel worthwhile.

Jan Yager[3]

GETTING IT ALL

together

TWELVE

We discover new parts of ourselves with our friends, who see us in different ways, touch aspects of ourselves we didn't realize existed, and encourage the changing identities our families may resist.

Teri Apter and Ruthellen Josselson[1]

Often I hear women ask, "What would I do without my friends?" Good friends help us laugh; they allow us to grieve and cry; listen to us when we are happy, hurt, angry, or upset; they share ideas and plans about relationships, families, other friends, work, life. Supportive friends can help us do almost anything, from renovating houses to caring for a baby to giving advice about jobs and boyfriends to being a sounding board about our successes and failures. Indeed, healthy friendships may be one of the best things that can happen to us. Such relationships are joyful, pleasurable, fun, exciting, powerful, almost miraculous. Occasionally they save our lives.

Yet, contrary to what was just declared, there are women who believe that women's relationships can be dangerous, and that if they choose to have a close friend, there is a possibility they will get hurt. They imagine themselves trusting someone who might betray or abandon them, and they fear that they will experience great pain. While they want a friend to appreciate them, they are afraid that she may be judgmental and that they will feel the sting of her criticism more than they would from someone who is not a friend. They assume that they will be too sensitive and personalize what a friend says, and that they will be devastated.

Throughout this book we have acknowledged that women's friendships can be hindered by difficulties that are fairly common and widespread. We've recognized that one of the primary causes of these problems stems from hundreds of years of oppression and mistreatment of the female sex by cultures, institutions, men, and women themselves. We understand that many women have accepted, internalized, and even practiced the repressive traditions of their cultures, resulting in negative feelings toward their own sex and themselves. These attitudes are often reflected in how they treat one another.

Another stumbling block is triggered by women having unrealistic ideas and expectations about their relationships with one another. Since they share the same gender, they assume they will automatically and effortlessly be friends. This is similar to what women often expect from mother-daughter and sister-sister relationships—just because they share the same blood (see "Our Mother, Our First Friend" and "Our Sisters, Our Partners in Friendship").

All too often we take friendships for granted, believing that we don't have to make an effort or put in much energy, time, or resources to be a good friend or to have one. So we don't nurture or take care of our relationships, and before we know it, they have somehow slipped to "the back burner" of our lives. Most of us wouldn't do this with our children, our families, our spouses, our partners, our colleagues at work. Yet we easily and repeatedly do it with our friends. At times we let our relationships completely drift away because something "more important" comes along, like a love relationship, marriage, children, a job, even a pet. Needless to say, all of this adds up to a surefire formula for disappointment and failure in our friendships. As Karen Eng writes, "Female friendships must be the most oversimplified, trivialized, underappreciated, and misunderstood of relationships. Women's friendships are not taken seriously. Accordingly, when things go wrong, that too is not taken seriously and the consequences can be devastating."[2]

Fortunately there is good news as well. Many women who have experienced challenges and difficulties have found workable solutions, giving us confidence that we too can resolve some of the pitfalls we encounter. In the process, we may discover new ways of working through and transforming concerns that arise in our relationships. Without a doubt, we can avoid being disappointed by relationships that don't meet our expectations or that slip away. And we can reclaim the power of our friendships and make them better, stronger, more genuine.

We start by recognizing that meaningful friendships—the kind that you can count on—are not simple nor are they effortless. They can be challenging and complicated. But is there anything in life that doesn't take an effort or is completely trouble-free—marriage, families, love relationships, jobs, politics, religion, life, living? We also need to realize the importance of having a fairly clear sense of *who we are*. Friendships are enhanced when we know ourselves and have a sense of self-confidence. This is basic to resolving problems that emerge in relationships.

We saw in earlier chapters that rather than envying someone's talents and accomplishments, we can examine and improve our own skills. Instead of competing in a toxic way, we might try identifying and enhancing our abilities and then choose if and how to compete in a healthier manner. To avoid inappropriate anger, we will benefit if we recognize how we have been wounded and learn how to heal our pain. If someone walks all over us, we can establish boundaries based on who we are or who we want to be. And expressing our real feelings and needs is essential, because we are worthy people.

But, if we don't feel good about ourselves, we can do something about that too. Certainly, there are many helpful and valuable resources available such as counseling services, therapists, spiritual directors, support groups, health centers, and religious institutions. In addition to these, most women feel better about who they are if they do some kind of meaningful work, help a neighbor, sign up to do volunteer work, join a singing group, participate in sports, reach out to those in need. People who have a sense of compassion and are involved with caring for others almost always discover that they lose some of their fears, their insecurities, their "negative stuff" in the process. When we do feel good about ourselves, our whole outlook on life changes and we are better, more *mature* friends. Perhaps "mature" is another key word. When we are mature, we are more open, more willing to grow and change, more capable of developing our potential, more likely to have quality friendships.

Also we may want to clarify *what we mean* when we use the word "friend"—a word frequently used to describe a wide range of relationships. Sometimes we are talking about a person who is a soulmate and committed to our relationship; who is absolutely trustworthy; who understands and accepts us, and encourages us to grow. We use the same word to describe a casual relationship with only occasional, somewhat indifferent connections. And we call people "friends" just because they have been around for some time. Because there are so many types of friends as well as different stages and levels of friendship, it may be impractical, perhaps meaningless, to try to have one definition of friendship. But it is beneficial if we clarify what *we think* are key qualities in our friendships. Jan Yager writes: "One way that you might define a friend is by those qualities that are sought in a friend, such as commitment, self-disclosure, trust, honesty, and commonality."[3]

After working with women's issues for over thirty years, both personally and professionally, interviewing hundreds of women, undertaking months of study and research, and hearing women's stories, I've altered and clarified many of my ideas about what are important elements in women's friendships. In the process I've also discovered many ideas and suggestions about how we can "get it all together" and reclaim the power of our relationships.

Getting It All Together

· ·

Friendships between women are special. They shape who we are and who we are yet to be. They soothe our tumultuous inner world, fill the emotional gaps in our marriage, and help us remember who we really are.

Susan Hankinson, et al.[4]

Having positive, realistic, and dependable friendships is a great benefit to our emotional and physical health and certainly is a goal worth striving for. But like everything else that we value, it requires motivation, commitment, and hard work. Here is a list of questions and suggestions to consider that might help us get it all together.

Do you feel good about yourself?

In numerous conversations with women, one theme keeps coming up: If women have positive feelings about themselves, they will almost certainly feel positive about their relationships with other women. When we are somewhat satisfied (there's always room for improvement) with our capabilities and contributions, we will be more relaxed, happier, and stronger women—and much better friends. If we are confident, we will enjoy and appreciate other women, including their strong and weak points. We will be more able to let problems including negativity and complications roll off our backs. Counseling, therapy, support groups, learning new skills, going back to school, and doing volunteer work can help us feel better about who we are. A woman who feels good about herself is a great role model and a gift to everyone.

Are you able to listen—really listen?

We can strengthen our relationships by being good listeners. When we really hear what someone is saying, we can correct budding irritations before they burst into full bloom. Listening with an open mind to what a friend is saying without running it through a lot of filters, without thinking we know what she is going to say, or without imagining she will unfairly criticize us are good ways to improve communications with our friend. And should she say something critical about us, we need to listen carefully to her words and figure out if there is any truth to them. Perhaps we will learn something from this exchange and make changes, if necessary. When I was a teenager, my mother said, "Joy, if you would just listen carefully, you wouldn't be in half so much trouble." The same principle applies for our interactions with friends.

Do you know how to make friends?

Old friends are wonderful, but they may leave us. They move, die, become ill, or get involved in an all-consuming activity that doesn't allow time for us. It's a good idea to make new friends on an ongoing basis. We can find friends who will help us stay more balanced, who will enjoy working or playing with us, and who will give us what we need. Are we looking for a spiritual friend, a serious sports woman, an environmentalist, an avid reader, a film buff, or a hiker? It will probably take an investment of our time and effort, but once we know what we want, we may be able to find someone we're looking for by joining special interest groups or organizations; by going to a continuing education program; by linking up with a church, religious organization, or volunteer group; by searching the Internet; or by just asking around. I know a woman who makes friends in front of the vegetables at the supermarket. She starts by asking questions. She has met a lot of people that way. Another woman meets women at the coffee shop in her favorite bookstore—they are passionate readers. It's worth trying whatever works.

Can you diversify your friendships and let
go of the idea of only having one "best friend"?

Some women have unrealistic expectations about a "best friend" being all things for them. But that's just not possible.

No one can be all things to any one person, be it friend, sister, spouse, or parent. Many women end up being frustrated, disappointed, and sometimes dumped, because one friend really can't meet all their needs. With friendship, as well as in other aspects of life, it's better not to put all of our eggs in one basket. There are many levels and flavors of friendship, and we might want to try sampling them. We can broaden our horizons by having friends of different ages, races, religions, sexes, and economic statuses. We may enjoy some of the new flavors more than we do the old ones. Not every friend has to be emotionally or geographically close to us. My friend Helen's three "best" friends are thirty-three, forty-three, and sixty-eight and are very different individuals. They have shared the ups and downs of her life and are always there for her. As I travel in my work, I meet and enjoy interesting women in many places. My "closest friends" live not only in the New York area, but in California, Colorado, Florida, Massachusetts, Nebraska, New Hampshire, New Jersey, North Carolina, Texas, Virginia, England, France, Greece, and Ireland.

*Are you aware that a healthy
friendship isn't just about feeling good?*

Many people do not respect or take seriously the value of women's friendships. Often they are viewed as frivolous, inconsequential, amusing, or even silly. But healthy female relationships are not just about having fun, feeling good, or being entertained. They provide a protected space to come into contact with and work out life's struggles, conflicts, and tough encounters. They are also testing grounds for learning difficult and complex lessons, for working through problems such as envy, toxic competition, anger, aggression, and boundary issues. They also offer a great place to grow and mature.

Can you clearly see your "friends" for who they really are?

Women who can realistically recognize who is or is not a friend are less likely to be disappointed by less-than-satisfying relationships. Sometimes what we *think* are "friends" really aren't, and it may be difficult to pinpoint what they actually are. Some women can be counted on through good and bad times. They talk over things when something goes awry, they understand us when we aren't at our best, and they can easily handle changes in the relationship. Other "friends" may be women that we've grown accustomed to having around, even though they might not be very supportive or truthful with us. Still others are essentially givers of pain and negative energy, although we may label them as friends. We might want to take a hard look at this last category and reflect on whether we should shake the dust off our feet and move on.

Are you willing to stay, rather than
running away, when things aren't going well?

Friendships, like life, are imperfect, inconsistent, and contain good and bad qualities. Many women aren't willing to deal with tough times, confront problems openly, or work through difficult dilemmas that may arise in their relationships. Their pride, guilt, shame, and fear get in the road. If a friend says something we don't like, even if they didn't mean to hurt us, our pride can be hurt and we may shut down. Or if we do something to a friend that we really shouldn't have done, we may have such guilt that we think we should disappear. But if we stick around long enough to investigate the situation and understand what's going on, we may discover that barriers which seemed insurmountable can be worked out. We may find that the relationship is worth saving. By thoughtfully assessing the situation, rather than just running away, our overall perspective about friendship may change.

Can you give up the tendency to assume?

Many women get into trouble by making assumptions. They assume too much and therefore end up being hurt about things that aren't correct or accurate or that have nothing to do with them. For example, when a friend whispers to someone, they assume that she is talking about them in a bad way. If a friend gets a nasty look on her face, they assume they have done something wrong and she is upset with them. Whenever we feel ourselves assuming the worst, we need to stop and give things a chance to unfold. Breathing deeply, asking questions, listening to what was said, pausing to mull things over, and using good judgment are much better solutions than assuming.

Can you make the most of
the changing dimensions of friendships?

We live in very transient times, and we experience many changes on our journey of life. Not only are women altering who they are, they are also changing their lifestyles, their jobs, their love relationships, and where they live. Long ago, it was almost impossible to stay in touch with a friend who moved across the state or across the country. But today, we can easily keep regular contact with our friends who move away through e-mail and relatively inexpensive long-distance phone rates. And we can save our money, watch for special travel deals, and visit friends who live far away. So it's possible to keep and enjoy our friendships, even when they are in another part of the world.

Can you recognize if someone is projecting
their stuff on you or when you are projecting yours on them?

When people project, they see a part of themselves in another person. They view someone else's behavior based on what they may wish they could do but can't. If people are hurting us without a real reason or falsely accusing us of something that has nothing to do with us, this probably isn't about us. It could be their problem or their "stuff" which they are projecting onto us. It's helpful if we don't personalize it or let it hurt us. And when we feel particularly critical of someone and what they are doing wrong, we may want to do a little checkup on ourselves. Perhaps we are projecting our stuff onto them. If so, we need to own our feelings and make amends.

Do you have thick enough skin?

Because women are supposed to be nice, pleasant, polite, and gentle, they tend to be people-pleasers who overreact to anything that doesn't appear to be complimentary of them. So they easily get their feelings hurt. If we have this problem, we may want to work at de-sensitizing ourselves and try to let certain words and actions roll off our backs rather than taking them personally. Every comment is not "about us" or a terrible injury to us, so we don't need to feel inadequate (if we do, we need to deal with our inadequacies in a healthy way). At other times if harsh words are used, we have to learn to shake them off and think about the intention behind the words. We might want to remind ourselves again that some negative comments aimed at us may be another person's misdirected feelings about themselves. And, we don't need to apologize for something someone *has done to us.* "I'm sorry" should be used only if *we* have done something unkind or insensitive to someone else.

Can you recognize when a relationship is unhealthy?

It's very hard to give up on what we want to believe is a friendship. Even though the relationship is harmful, we may be afraid there won't be another "friend" to replace this one. Often we think someone who has been around for a while is a friend. But that's not necessarily true. I admit I've been a qualified "offender" of this practice. For years, I didn't easily or willingly give up on any relationship even when I knew it wasn't working for me or for the other woman. If we have tried to make a relationship work, but we know it is unhealthy, even toxic, it's much better to acknowledge and accept it for what it is. And then we can let it go—with kindness and gentleness. Talking about what happened is helpful and less hurtful than just walking away, but it takes courage. When we just slip away, we can hurt one another and end up having regrets. And let's never send a "Dear Jane" letter; it's not something anyone should do to their worst enemy. These letters don't close doors—they smack the recipient in the face!

Are you willing to swallow your pride
and forgive—both your friends and yourself?

Psychologists point out that it's not unusual for people who have little self-worth or are hurting to inflict pain on others. If a friend hurts us, we should aim to take the high road and try to be understanding, non-judgmental, and kind. By going a step further and forgiving her, we may free ourselves of the burden of carrying around extra baggage. If we are able to forgive ourselves, it is easier to forgive our friends and to feel better about ourselves. At times, we may be the person who needs to ask for forgiveness for inflicting our own brokenness on someone. Remember that Jesus, who was ruthlessly humiliated and wounded, compassionately said from the cross, "Forgive them for they know not what they do."

Are you able to practice up-front frankness with kindness?

If we aren't able to be truthful with our friends, we likely will have rather weak, artificial friendships that won't stand the test of time. That might not be what we really want. But candor and straightforwardness require some caution signs. If they are not wrapped in compassion, we run the risk of being hurtful, insensitive, and inconsiderate. No one has the right to injure someone with "brutal honesty," which can be cruel and damaging. Practicing truthfulness with kindness is a much nobler thing to do. So let's speak what's in our hearts gently, but honestly.

Do you have a sense of humor?

We know that laughter is very good medicine; in fact, it does help people heal. If we can learn how to face problems with an *appropriate* sense of humor and laugh at some of our absurd reactions and less-than-wise endeavors, we may find that we have put on an "armor" of humor and love that will protect us from a lot of anguish and grief while giving joy to others and to ourselves.

Are you able to be flexible?

Women who are flexible can let go of their expectations about how a friendship should be shaped. Their relationships tend to be more relaxed, enjoyable, and satisfying. Rather than rigidly trying to make things come out "perfectly" or trying to be the "perfect" friend, they accept themselves—and their friends—for who and what they are. If we can be flexible and open to women we meet—even though they might not meet our "requirements" for friendship, we will have opportunities to establish some surprisingly pleasant relationships. It's also important for us to let a relationship unfold and to accept it for the way it is, because *that's the way it is.* On the flip side, we want to choose friends who are flexible, who can roll with things, and who don't want us to be someone other than who we are.

Do you appreciate your friends?

Friends are very important to our emotional and physical health. Yet too often we take them for granted. Friends are far too precious not to value and treasure. And like almost everything in life, our friends will someday be gone, too. If we can savor every minute of our friendships and appreciate our friends while they are in our lives, we will not have regrets later.

Are you open to new ideas about friendship?

When I started working on this book, I had been involved for several decades with women and their issues—both in the United States and in countries around the world. I thought I knew almost everything there was to know about women's relationships. But I didn't. I've gained a lot of knowledge, and I see whole new aspects about women's relationships that I didn't know existed. Sometimes new ideas or a change in perspective may seem frightening to us. But if we are open to approaching relationships with a fresh start and some new ideas, we may have opportunities to experience some of life's little surprises: new understandings about friendship, new ways of relating to old friends, and new friendships.

What would our lives have been like without these relationships, these women who came into our lives at just the right moment? Many times we feel that our friends are sent to us from heaven.

Carmen Renee Berry and Tamara Traeder[5]

Without a doubt, having meaningful, healthy relationships with women can be a challenge. Friendships usually require patience, commitment, maturity, loyalty, responsibility, and effort—just as any relationship does with partners, spouses, parents, children, or professional colleagues. We know that anything that is valuable or important to us has a price tag; it does not come free. But once we truly reach the point of having a genuine friendship, we will find that the returns are satisfying. An authentic friendship is awe-inspiring. It can give us joy, energy, optimism, new hope, and new dreams.

• •

A friend is one who knows you as you are and understands where you've been, accepts who you've become and still, gently invites you to grow.

Anonymous

TEN STEPS TO

better

friendships

APPENDIX

Real friends are there for each other whenever they are needed, to share triumphs and failures, laughter and tears. They want the best for each other, and they encourage one another to pursue their dreams and to find fulfillment in their lives. A quality friendship between women offers ongoing support, confidence, and many learning experiences. Good friends don't have to worry that they will be misunderstood or disliked if they are too powerful or too weak, too attractive or too unattractive. They allow each other to be completely themselves. Their relationships weather all kinds of differences, changes, craziness, and transformations.

But meaningful friendships—the kind you can truly count on—are not simple or effortless. At times, they can be complicated and challenging. Here are ten qualities that you may want to cultivate that will help you have more lasting friendships.

1. *Know yourself.* Self-awareness is a key ingredient to experiencing lasting friendships. When you know yourself you can be more comfortable with yourself. Thus you can have positive feelings about other women and your relationships with them. When you are satisfied with your capabilities and contributions, you are more relaxed and stronger. If you are confident, you are able to enjoy and appreciate other women and let insignificant problems roll off your back.

2. *Be flexible.* Women who are flexible can let go of their expectations about how a friendship should be shaped. Rather than rigidly trying to make things come out "perfectly," they accept themselves—and their friends—for who and what they are. Their relationships tend to be

more relaxed, enjoyable, and satisfying. If you can be flexible and open to women you meet—even though they might not meet your "requirements" for friendship, you will have opportunities to establish some surprisingly pleasant relationships.

3. *Listen—really listen.* Try listening with an open mind to what a friend is saying without running the words through filters, without thinking you know what she is going to say, or without imagining she will unfairly criticize you. And if she does say something critical about you, try to listen carefully to her words and figure out if there is any truth in them.

4. *Diversify your friendships.* Many women end up being disappointed, and sometimes dumped, because they have unrealistic expectations about a "best friend" who will meet all their needs. No one person can meet all of our needs. There are many levels and flavors of friendship, and you might want to try sampling them by branching out, broadening your horizons, and having friends of different ages, races, religions, sexes, and economic status. You may be surprised that you will enjoy some of the new flavors more than the old ones.

5. *Avoid assuming.* Many women end up being hurt because they make assumptions about things that aren't correct or have nothing to do with them. For example, when a friend whispers to someone, they assume that she is talking about them—in a bad way. Whenever you feel yourself assuming the worst, stop and give things a chance to unfold. Breathe deeply, ask questions, listen to what was said, pause to mull things over.

6. *Don't run away.* Friendships are not perfect. Many times we aren't willing to deal with tough times or confront problems openly. Our pride and fear get in the way. When your pride is hurt you may want to shut down. If you feel guilty, you may want to disappear. But if you stick around long enough to understand what's going on, you may discover that barriers that seemed insurmountable really aren't.

7. *Be truthful, but kind.* If you aren't truthful with your friends, your friendships will likely be rather artificial. They won't stand the test of time. But candor and straightforwardness require caution and care. If they are not wrapped in compassion and gentleness, you run the risk of being hurtful. No one has the right to use "brutal honesty." Try to speak what's in your heart gently, but truthfully.

8. *Have a sense of humor.* Laughter is good medicine; in actual fact, it does help people heal. If you can learn how to face problems with an appropriate sense of humor and laugh at yourself, you may find that you'll avoid a lot of anguish and grief. And you'll be a source of joy and pleasure to others!

9. *Learn to be tough enough.* Try to not let words and actions that aren't positive have an impact on you. Don't take them personally or allow them to hurt you. Think about what may have been the intention behind the words. And remember that sometimes negative comments aimed at you are really the other person's less-than-positive feelings about herself being misdirected at you.

10. *Swallow your pride.* Although it's difficult to do, when a friend hurts you, first try to take the high road and understand what is happening without being judgmental. If you can go a step further and forgive her, you may free yourself of the burden of carrying around extra baggage. Remember, there may come a time when you will be the person who needs to ask for forgiveness.

BIBLIOGRAPHY

Alpert, Barbara, ed. *The Love of Friends: A Celebration of Women's Friendship*. New York: Berkeley Books, 1997.

Angier, Natalie. *Woman: An Intimate Geography*. New York: Anchor, 2000.

Apter, Terri and Ruthellen Josselson. *Best Friends: The Pleasures and Perils of Girls' and Women's Friendships*. New York: Three Rivers Press, 1998.

de Beauvoir, Simone. *The Second Sex*. New York: Vintage, 1989.

Bernay, Toni and Dorothy Cantor, eds. *The Psychology of Today's Woman: New Psychoanalytic Visions*. Hillsdale, NJ: Analytic Press, 1986.

Berry, Carmen Renee and Tamara Traeder. *Girlfriends: Invisible Bonds, Enduring Ties*. Berkeley: Wildcat Canyon Press, 1995.

Berry, Carmen Renee and Tamara Traeder. *Girlfriends for Life: Friendships Worth Keeping Forever*. Berkeley: Wildcat Canyon Press, 1998.

Braiker, Harriet B. *The Disease to Please: Curing the People-Pleasing Syndrome*. New York: McGraw-Hill, 2001.

Brestin, Dee. *The Friendships of Women: Harnessing the Power in Our Heartwarming, Heartrending Relationships*. Colorado Springs: Chariot Victor Publishing, 1997.

Brothers, Joyce. "That Green-Eyed Monster—and What to Do About Him!" *Good Housekeeping* 169 (August 1969), 46.

Bucklin, Linda and Mary Keil. *Come Rain or Come Shine: Friendships between Women*. Holbrook, MA: Adams Media Corporation, 1999.

Burbank, Victoria K. "Cross-cultural perspectives on aggression in women and girls: An introduction." *Behavior Science Research*, 1987.

Chesler, Phyllis. *Woman's Inhumanity to Woman*. New York: Plume Book, 2003.

Cloud, Henry and John Townsend. *Boundaries: When to Say Yes, When to Say No to Take Control of Your Life*. Grand Rapids, MI: Zondervan, 1992.

Cloud, Henry and John Townsend. *Safe People: How to Find Relationships That Are Good for You and Avoid Those That Aren't*. Grand Rapids, MI: Zondervan, 1995.

Cohen, Betsy. *The Snow White Syndrome: All About Envy.* New York: Macmillan Publishing, 1986.

Downing, Christine. *Psyche's Sisters: Re-imagining the Meaning of Sisterhood.* San Francisco: Harper and Row, 1988.

Eichenbaum, Luise and Susie Orbach. *Between Women: Love, Envy and Competition in Women's Friendships.* New York: Penguin Books, 1988.

Eng, Karen, ed. *Secrets and Confidences: The Complicated Truth about Women's Friendships.* Emeryville, CA: Seal Press/Avalon Publishing, 2004.

Evans, Gail. *Play Like a Man, Win like a Woman: What Men Know about Success that Women Need to Learn.* New York: Broadway Books, 2000.

Firman, Julie and Dorothy Firman. *Daughters and Mothers: Healing the Relationship.* New York: Continuum, 1989.

Friday, Nancy. *My Mother/My Self: The Daughter's Search for Identity.* New York: Delta, 1997.

Gallagher, BJ. *Everything I Need to Know I Learned from Other Women.* York Beach, ME: Conari Press, 2002.

Galland, China. *The Bond Between Women: A Journey to Fierce Compassion.* New York: Riverhead Books, 1998.

Gerard, Robert V. *Handling Verbal Confrontation: Take the Fear Out of Facing Others.* Coarsegold, CA: Oughten House Foundation, Inc. 1999.

Goodman, Ellen and Patricia O'Brien. *I Know Just What You Mean: The Power of Friendship in Women's Lives.* New York: Fireside Book/Simon and Schuster, 2000.

Gray, John. *Men Are from Mars, Women Are from Venus: A Practical Guide for Improving Communication and Getting What You Want in Your Relationships.* New York: HarperCollins, 1992.

Hales, Dianne. *Just Like a Woman.* New York: Bantam Paperback, 2000.

Hankinson, Susan E., Graham A. Colditz, JoAnn E. Manson, and Frank E. Speizer. *Healthy Women, Healthy Lives: A Guide to Preventing Disease, from the Landmark Nurses' Health Study.* Harvard Medical School Book. New York: Fireside Book/Simon & Schuster, 2002.

Hansen, Suzy. "A Girl's Best Friend." *New York Times Book Review,* May 22, 2005.

Howard, Jane. *Families.* Somerset, NJ: Transaction Publishers, 1998.

Kohn, Alfie, *No Contest: The Case Against Competition.* Boston: Houghton Mifflin Company, 1986.

Kolbenschlag, Madonna. *Kiss Sleeping Beauty Goodbye: Breaking the Spell of Feminine Myths and Models*. San Francisco: HarperSanFrancisco, 1988.

Lerner, Harriet Goldhor. *The Dance of Intimacy: A Woman's Guide to Courageous Acts of Change in Key Relationships*. New York: Harper and Row, 1989.

Loden, Marilyn. *Feminine Leadership*. New York: Crown, 1985.

Mathias, Barbara. *Between Sisters*. New York: Delta Books, 1992.

McClure, Judith Selee. *Civilized Assertiveness for Women: Communication with Backbone . . . not Bite*. Denver: Albion Street Press, 2003.

Morgenstern, Mindy. *The Real Rules for Girls*. New York: Pocket, 2002.

O'Connor, Pat. *Friendships Between Women: A Critical Review*. New York: The Guilford Press, 1992.

Offill, Jenny and Elissa Schappell, eds. *The Friend Who Got Away: Twenty Women's True-Life Tales of Friendships That Blew Up, Burned Out, or Faded Away*. New York: Doubleday, 2005.

Reilly, Patricia Lynn. *Imagine a Woman in Love with Herself: Embracing Your Wisdom and Wholeness*. Berkeley: Conari Press, 1999.

Rubin, Lillian. *Just Friends: The Role of Friendship in Our Lives*. New York: Harper and Row, 1985.

Sanford, Barbara, ed. *On Being Female: An Anthology*. New York: Washington Square Press, 1974.

Schlessinger, Laura. *10 Stupid Things Women Do to Mess up Their Lives*. New York: Quill, 1995.

Secund, Victoria. *Women and Their Fathers: The Sexual and Romantic Impact of the First Man in Your Life*. New York: Delta, 1993.

Sheehy, Sandy. *Connecting: The Enduring Power of Female Friendship*. New York: William Morrow, 2000.

Simmons, Rachel. *Odd Girl Out: The Hidden Culture of Aggression in Girls*. New York: Harvest Books/Harcourt, 2002.

Stoddard, Alexandra. *Living Beautifully Together*. New York: Doubleday, 1989.

Tracy, Laura. *The Secret between Us: Competition among Women*. Boston: Little, Brown, 1991.

Tutu, Archbishop Desmond. *No Future Without Forgiveness*. New York: Doubleday, 1999.

Ulanov, Ann and Barry Ulanov. *Cinderella and Her Sisters: The Envied and the Envying*. Quebec: Daimon Verlag, 1998.

Wiseman, Rosalind. *Queen Bees and Wannabes: Helping Your Daughter Survive Cliques, Gossip, Boyfriends and Other Realities of Adolescence.* New York: Three Rivers Press, 2002.

Yager, Jan. *Friendshifts: The Power of Friendship and How It Shapes Our Lives.* Stamford, CT: Hannacroix Creek Books, Inc., 1999.

Yager, Jan. *When Friendship Hurts: How to Deal with Friends Who Betray, Abandon, or Wound You.* New York: Fireside Book/Simon and Schuster, 2002.

NOTES

Chapter 1

1. Berg, *New Woman*, in Alpert, ed., *The Love of Friends*, 101.
2. Kidd in Berry and Traeder, *Girlfriends*, 8–9.
3. Howard, *Families.*
4. Hankinson, Colditz, Manson, and Speizer, *Healthy Women, Healthy Lives.*
5. Chesler, *Woman's Inhumanity to Woman.*
6. Stoddard, *Living Beautifully Together*, in Alpert, *The Love of Friends*, 4.

Chapter 2

1. Yager, *Friendshifts*, 199.
2. Firman and Firman, *Daughters and Mothers*, xi.
3. Friday, *My Mother/My Self*, 98.
4. Secund, *Women and Their Fathers*, chapter 3.
5. Herman and Lewis, "Anger in the mother-daughter relationship," in Bernay and Cantor, eds., *Psychology of Today's Woman.*
6. Cohen, *The Snow White Syndrome*, 68.
7. Chesler, *Woman's Inhumanity to Woman*, 217.
8. Firman and Firman, *Daughters and Mothers*, xii.
9. Tutu, *No Future Without Forgiveness*, 273.
10. Lerner, *The Dance of Intimacy*, 184.

Chapter 3

1. Mathias, *Between Sisters*, 273.
2. Berry and Traeder, *Girlfriends*, 140.
3. Mathias, *Between Sisters*, 11.
4. Downing, *Psyche's Sisters*, in Chesler, *Woman's Inhumanity to Woman*, 292.
5. Ibid.
6. Fishel, in Berry and Traeder, *Girlfriends*, 137.

Chapter 4

1. Cohen, *The Snow White Syndrome*, 170.
2. Ulanov and Ulanov. *Cinderella and Her Sisters.*
3. Cohen, *The Snow White Syndrome*, 20–21.
4. Kolbenschlag, *Kiss Sleeping Beauty Goodbye*, in Cohen, *The Snow White Syndrome*, 164.
5. Brothers, "That Green-Eyed Monster," 46.

Chapter 5

1. Simmons, *Odd Girl Out*, 118.
2. Eichenbaum and Orbach, *Between Women*, 114.
3. Tracy, *The Secret Between Us.*
4. Wiseman, *Queen Bees and Wannabes*, 114.
5. Rubin, *Just Friends*, 83, 89.
6. Ibid., 83.
7. Eichenbaum and Orbach, *Between Women*, 126.

Chapter 6

1. Yager, *When Friendship Hurts*, 75.
2. Eichenbaum and Orbach, *Between Women*, 135.
3. Burbank, "Cross-cultural perspectives on aggression in women and girls."
4. Angier, *Woman*, in Chesler, *Woman's Inhumanity to Woman*, 77.
5. Chesler, *Woman's Inhumanity to Woman*, 83.
6. Ibid., 36–37.
7. Eichenbaum and Orbach, *Between Women*, 142.

Chapter 7

1. Evans, *Play Like a Man*, 26.
2. Hales, *Just Like a Woman.*
3. Chesler, *Woman's Inhumanity to Woman*, 357.
4. Loden, *Feminine Leadership*, in Gallagher, *Everything I Need to Know*, 172.
5. Gallagher, *Everything I Need to Know*, 167.
6. Kohn, *No Contest.*
7. Berry and Traeder, *Girlfriends*, 171.

Chapter 8

1. McClure, *Civilized Assertiveness for Women*, 73.
2. Cloud and Townsend, *Safe People*, 73.
3. Braiker, *The Disease to Please*, 6.
4. Ibid., 17.
5. Ibid., 49.
6. Cloud and Townsend, *Boundaries*, 29.

Chapter 9

1. de Beauvoir, *The Second Sex*, 345.
2. Ibid., 604.
3. Ibid., 335.
4. Apter and Josselson, *Best Friends*, 244.
5. Ibid., 248.
6. Ibid., 253.
7. Yager, *Friendshifts*, 83.

Chapter 10

1. Eichenbaum and Orbach, *Between Women*, 147.
2. Reilly, *Imagine a Woman*, 71.
3. McClure, *Civilized Assertiveness for Women*, 21.
4. Eichenbaum and Orbach, *Between Women*, 149.
5. Prose, in Offill and Schappell, *The Friend Who Got Away*, xx.
6. Hansen, "A Girl's Best Friend," 8.
7. Eichenbaum and Orbach, *Between Women*, 167.
8. McClure, *Civilized Assertiveness for Women*, 2.
9. Gallagher, *Everything I Need to Know*, 200.
10. Reilly, *Imagine a Woman*, 75.

Chapter 11

1. Gallagher, *Everything I Need to Know*, 30.
2. Ibid.
3. Yager, *Friendshifts*, 5.

Chapter 12

1. Apter and Josselson, *Best Friends*, 275.
2. Eng, ed., *Secrets and Confidences*, viii–ix.
3. Yager, *Friendshifts*, 15–16.
4. Hankinson, Colditz, Manson, and Speizer, *Healthy Women, Healthy Lives*.
5. Berry and Traeder, *Girlfriends for Life*, 33.

JOY CAROL is an author, speaker, counselor, and spiritual director. She leads retreats and workshops across the country on a variety of topics, including women's issues. Founder of the Union Center for Women and co-author of the official report on the United Nations' Decade for Women, Carol also was an international consultant on women and development for the Ford Foundation, Save the Children, the UN, and other international organizations. She is a member of the Women's International League for Peace & Freedom and an active volunteer for the American Red Cross and Habitat for Humanity.

Carol holds an honorary doctorate from Nebraska Wesleyan University and master's degrees from the General Theological Seminary of New York and the University of Maryland.

Other books by Carol include *Towers of Hope: Stories to Help Us Heal* (Forest of Peace), *Journeys of Courage: Remarkable Stories of the Healing Power of Community* (Sorin Books), *Finding Courage* (Veritas Publications), and *You Don't Have to Be Rich to Own a Brownstone* (Quadrangle Books). She has also written numerous articles on women's issues.

Nurturing a Woman's Soul

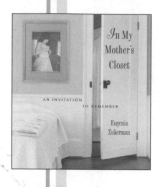

In My Mother's Closet
An Invitation to Remember
Eugenia Zukerman
Share laughter, tears, and loving resolutions as over forty accomplished women share memories of their mothers' closets, where they tried on clothes, jewelry, and shoes—and imagined the world they would enter: the world of being a woman.
ISBN: 1-893732-47-9 / 256 pages, hardcover / $24.95 / Sorin Books

Loving Yourself More
101 Meditations for Women
Virginia Ann Froehle, R.S.M.
Froehle invites women to dwell on the most basic of all Christian truths: God's love for us and God's call for us to love ourselves. She adapts the scriptures so that they speak personally to women.
ISBN: 0-87793-513-0 / 128 pages / $8.95 / Ave Maria Press

The Circle of Life
The Heart's Journey Through the Seasons
Joyce Rupp and Macrina Wiederkehr
Artwork by Mary Southard
Reflections, poems, prayers, and meditations help readers to explore the relationship between the seasons of the earth and the seasons of their lives. Discover the seasons as stepping-stones along the path of the great circle of life, and guides for life's journey.
ISBN 1-893732-82-7 / 288 pages / $19.95 / Sorin Books

AmP
ave maria press

Available from your local bookstore or from **ave maria press**
Notre Dame, IN 46556 / www.avemariapress.com
ph: 1.800.282.1865 / fax: 1.800.282.5681
Prices and availability subject to change.

Keycode: FØTØ5Ø6ØØØØ